ONLY IN
CHICAGO

ONLY IN
CHICAGO

HOW THE **ROD BLAGOJEVICH SCANDAL** ENGULFED
ILLINOIS AND ENTHRALLED THE NATION

NATASHA KORECKI

MIDWAY

AN AGATE IMPRINT

CHICAGO

Printed in the United States of America.

Photos reprinted with permission from the *Chicago Sun-Times*.

Library of Congress Cataloging-in-Publication Data

Korecki, Natasha.
Only in Chicago : how the Rod Blagojevich scandal engulfed Illinois; embroiled Barack Obama, Rahm Emanuel, and Jesse Jackson, Jr.; and enthralled the nation / Natasha Korecki.
    p. cm.
Includes index.
    ISBN 978-1-57284-144-4 (pbk.) -- ISBN 1-57284-144-3 (paperback) -- ISBN 978-1-57284-425-4 (ebook)
1. Blagojevich, Rod R., 1956---Trials, litigation, etc. 2. Political corruption--Illinois. 3. Illinois--Politics and government--1951- 4. Obama, Barack 5. Emanuel, Rahm, 1959- 6. Jackson, Jesse, 1965- I. Title.
F546.4.B55K67 2013
977.3'044092--dc23
                                    2013019283

10 9 8 7 6 5 4 3 2 1

Midway is an imprint of Agate Publishing. Agate books are available in bulk at discount prices. For more information, visit agatepublishing.com.

I dedicate this book as I do everything in life, to my three dear loves:
Bob, Daniel, and Cormac.

Contents

Prologue

On my second day on the job at the *Chicago Sun-Times* in 2004, I was asked to run over to the federal courthouse to back up another reporter. Two governors later, I was still on the beat.

In my time in the Dirksen Federal Courthouse, I've seen a healthy variety of disgraced public officials, public workers, businessmen, and private citizens stand before judges and face charges. From 2005 to 2006, I covered what was then considered a historic trial: that of former Governor George Ryan. Amazingly, a few years later, a different governor—one who had run on the platform of reform—was standing in front of me in a criminal courtroom.

That's one of the reasons that *Only in Chicago* seemed such a fitting title for this book. Even before the Rod Blagojevich case came along, there were times when I felt I could end the story I was writing for the newspaper with those three words.

But after Blagojevich was charged in 2008, it became clear this case was unlike anything the state had ever seen. I began writing "The Blago Blog," for the *Sun-Times*, where I detailed day-to-day happenings on the investigation into Blagojevich and others, and documented Blagojevich's trips to court, his bizarre news conferences, and his brush with reality TV. I later reported on both

Blagojevich's first trial and his retrial for the *Sun-Times*, where we fed readers' appetites for instant news. That often meant giving up-to-the-minute updates on the blog and Twitter. Getting it down in real time in such detail helped immensely when I got a call in December of 2011 from Doug Seibold, the president of Agate Publishing, expressing interest in a Blagojevich book.

The case of Rod Blagojevich was stunning in and of itself, but there's something people too often overlook. Blagojevich didn't operate in a vacuum. Blagojevich had advisers and ex-advisers who were willing to feed his ego and egg him on, or, at the very least, who weren't brave enough to tell him when he had strayed way off course.

Blagojevich's power in the state diminished as it became well known that his administration was under federal scrutiny. But once it was clear that he had the power to appoint Barack Obama's successor as U.S. senator from Illinois, there were plenty of people whose political aspirations drew them too close to the Blagojevich fire. Not surprisingly, many of them got burned. Close advisers and fundraisers were charged and convicted. They saw prison time. The political careers of those who weren't charged—some of the most powerful men in the country—were forever tainted. That included Roland Burris, Blagojevich's eventual appointment to the U.S. Senate, and U.S. Rep. Jesse Jackson Jr., who had repeatedly tried to outrun the dark cloud that the Blagojevich case cast over him.

Plenty of others were politically singed. Obama himself called a union rep the day before he was elected to be leader of the free world, to give him the OK to talk to Blagojevich about his friend Valerie Jarrett for appointment to his Senate seat. Rahm Emanuel, then an outgoing U.S. congressman and incoming White House chief of staff, was caught on tape trying to handpick his own successor.

About 30 percent of this book uses material as it appeared on the blog or in the paper.

In other cases, I obtained copies of court transcripts, conducted follow-up interviews, rewrote other passages, and dug down for more details to flesh out other parts of the story. In the chapters involving Christopher Kelly and Jesse Jackson Jr., I used a research assistant, Lark Turner, who covered the second Blagojevich trial with me as part of an internship at the *Sun-Times*. We relied heavily on the police report involving Kelly's death. I also attended Kelly's funeral as a reporter for the newspaper.

In the Jackson and Burris chapters, I drew information from a series of interviews I conducted while working with the *Sun-Times*. For the reader's sake, I do not end various paragraphs with "sources said," in those chapters or in others, so as not to slow down the narrative with repeated attribution.

Besides covering these events in real time as a reporter for the *Sun-Times*, I have interviewed more than 100 people, including central players in the scandal, throughout my time covering Blagojevich and the related investigations. I've obtained hundreds of documents in that time and gone over dozens of recordings, phone records, and official government schedules as well as emails and transcripts.

Cast of Characters: All the Governor's Men

Rod Blagojevich: Elected governor of Illinois in 2002 and 2006, he ran for office after holding elected positions in the Illinois statehouse as well as the U.S. Congress. Early in his career as governor he raised heaps of campaign cash at lightning speed, and soon he was under scrutiny for handing out positions in his administration in exchange for campaign donations. In a spectacular wiretap investigation, Blagojevich was subsequently accused of trying to sell Barack Obama's vacant Senate seat.

Barack Obama: U.S. senator from Illinois whose election to the presidency meant the remaining term on his Senate seat would be filled by appointment. Obama's political ascent launched a flurry of horse-trading and jockeying to be named to replace him. The person with the sole power to appoint his successor was the governor of Illinois—Rod Blagojevich.

Christopher Kelly: The owner of a roofing company, he was the unlikely co-architect of Blagojevich's fundraising strategies. He became known as the governor's go-to money guy and was accused of demanding campaign contributions from firms that wanted to do business with the state. An avid gambler, he was named by Blagojevich to head up Illinois gaming issues. He was indicted three times before he ultimately took his own life.

Tony Rezko: A Syrian national with a rags-to-riches life story, this deep-pocketed businessman was known for his ability to pick political rising stars. Once a friend and donor to Barack Obama, Rezko likewise befriended Blagojevich and quickly grew to be a close adviser, strategist, and fundraiser. He was accused of controlling state boards along with Stuart Levine and of scheming to get kickbacks from state deals. He was convicted in 2008 and is serving a ten-and-a-half-year prison sentence.

Stuart Levine: Wealthy North Shore-based member of the Illinois Health Facilities Planning Board and the Teachers Retirement System (TRS) board, he was also a serial scam artist who led a secret life that involved snorting crystal meth at a sketchy suburban Chicago hotel in all-night drug parties with other men. A wiretap on his phone revealed he was scheming to extract kickbacks in exchange for steering votes on the state boards. Levine, once worth

$70 million, personally knew some of the most significant backroom dealers in Illinois. Levine was the marquee witness against Rezko and, later, businessman William Cellini. Prosecutors called him one of the most significant cooperators in Chicago's federal courthouse in 30 years.

Valerie Jarrett: Adviser to Barack Obama who in the fall of 2008 was interested in replacing him as U.S. senator. Jarrett's interest prompted Blagojevich to make dozens of recorded phone calls plotting, and then asking an intermediary, for Obama to name him either to a cabinet post or an ambassadorship, or to head a nonprofit organization in exchange for appointing Jarrett to Obama's vacated seat.

Jesse Jackson Jr.: Ambitious son of the famed social activist, he pulled out all the stops in advocating for Blagojevich to appoint him to replace Obama in the U.S. Senate in 2008. Blagojevich is heard on tape saying he believed he would receive $1.5 million from Jackson supporters if the Chicago congressman were named to the Senate. Two people, Raghu Nayak and Rajinder Bedi, have told authorities that Jackson talked about raising money for Blagojevich in exchange for the appointment. Jackson has repeatedly denied this, in interviews and under oath.

Raghuveer (Raghu) Nayak: Close friend to the Jackson family, he once traveled to India with the Reverend Jesse Jackson and had a company with another Jackson son. Nayak was a wealthy member of a community of Indian-American donors and a major fundraiser for Jackson Jr. In October 2008, Nayak traveled to Washington, D.C., and met with Rep. Jackson. Nayak told authorities that Jackson had asked him to approach Blagojevich with a money offer in exchange for the U.S. Senate appointment. Nayak said the amount Jackson suggested was $6 million—not the $1.5 million that was often cited in the Blagojevich case. Nayak also told authorities there was more to Jackson's offer than money. Nayak did not testify at Blagojevich's trials; but Blagojevich appointee Rajinder Bedi did, and Bedi accused Nayak of laundering hundreds of thousands of dollars through him in an alleged check-cashing scheme.

Rajinder Bedi: Fundraiser who worked under Blagojevich as his managing director of the state's Office of Trade and Investment. Blagojevich referred to Bedi as "my Sikh warrior." Prosecutors said Bedi met with Rep. Jackson and Nayak on October 28, 2008, at a Chicago restaurant, and that at this meeting Nayak promised to raise $1 million for Blagojevich if he appointed Jackson to the Senate seat.

Robert "Rob" Blagojevich: The governor's brother, a banking professional who, but for a few brief stints, had mostly stayed out of his brother's affairs. Then, in August 2008, at Rod's request, he returned to Illinois from his home in Tennessee to run his brother's campaign fund. He was accused of trying to help his brother get something in exchange for the Senate seat appointment.

Lisa Madigan: Illinois attorney general and also the daughter of Blagojevich's biggest political nemesis, Illinois House Speaker Michael Madigan. Blagojevich's defense largely revolved around the theory that he had always intended to appoint her to the Senate in exchange for her father's political support in pushing through the governor's legislative agenda.

Richard Mell: Father of Blagojevich's wife, Patti. A powerful Chicago alderman, he supplied the political muscle to put his son-in-law into public office. As Blagojevich's star rose, their relationship took a vicious, public plunge.

Chapter One

"Only in Chicago"

It was the fall of 2008 and the highest-ranking law enforcement agent in the country headed to the Windy City. Sensitive wiretaps were up, and FBI agents were covertly recording what could turn out to be a spectacular public corruption case. Chicago agents were working lengthy shifts, monitoring bugs and wired phones.

FBI Director Robert Mueller wanted to hear some of the tech cuts himself. Walking past piles of papers heaped on the desk of Robert Grant, Chicago FBI special agent in charge, in his near West Side office, Mueller settled in. He asked his bodyguards to leave the room. With only Mueller, Grant, and top FBI supervisor Pete Cullen left, the tapes rolled. Mueller, who has overseen numerous terrorism and corruption cases at the bureau, listened to the conversations for the first time.

He stopped and looked up. Who was dropping all those f-bombs? he asked.

That's the governor, he was told.

Mueller shook his head.

"Only in Chicago."

It's not just Chicagoans who are a hardened lot, but Illinoisans statewide. Between the politicos from Chicago and Springfield, there's not much they haven't seen.

Dead people cast votes. Truckers pay bribes to get their commercial driving licenses. An "honest" state official dies, and shoe-boxes stuffed with cash are found in his hotel suite. It's where a state court judge fixed a murder case. Where corpses were dug up, their bones put into a pile, their cemetery plots resold. And it's where governors go to prison.

Still, some might say the story of Rod Blagojevich is one in which the Land of Lincoln shifted—maybe even enough, as the onetime U.S. Attorney here famously said, to make our sixteenth president roll over in his grave.

On December 9, 2008, Illinois Governor Rod Blagojevich was arrested at his home, charged in a 76-page criminal complaint with trying to leverage personal gain for himself when given the sole power as governor to appoint a replacement for Barack Obama to the U.S. Senate. Blagojevich, who had been viewed as a young, dynamic reform candidate before he came into office, was accused of making various attempts to "sell" the Senate seat appointment for a variety of awards, including more than $1 million in campaign funds.

The charging documents were riddled with colorful language, not the least of which was Blagojevich's description of his new-found power to appoint. "I mean I, I've got this thing and it's fucking golden," he said on tape. "And I, I'm just not giving it up for fucking nothing." Public reaction was swift. *Saturday Night Live* aired a skit mocking the foul-mouthed Blagojevich and his wife, portraying them as money-hungry and corrupt. The Second City comedy troupe in Chicago put on a musical revue called *Rod Blagojevich Superstar*.

Blagojevich's arrest happened about one month after another historic event centered in Chicago—Obama became the first African American to be elected president. The complaint noted that Blagojevich had used the word "motherfucker" to refer to a fellow Illinois Democrat who had just made history. Obama's offense: he asked Blagojevich to appoint his successor, but promised him nothing in return. It was that kind of language that caused Mueller to shake his head in disbelief when listening to samples of the taped calls.

It turned out that Mueller's comment about Chicago was one he made pretty often. He'd needle his Windy City crew, telling them that charging public corruption in Chicago was like shooting fish in a barrel. This was hard to dispute. About a year before Blagojevich was in handcuffs, his predecessor as Illinois governor began his own prison sentence. The "Chicago Machine" has a long, storied history of corrupt dealings in the city and state. Besides the Senate seat affair, the remaining charges leveled against Blagojevich were astounding: trying to shake down a children's hospital for a campaign contribution; sitting on legislation that supported horseracing because a racetrack owner hadn't kicked in to his campaign kitty; plotting to get a newspaper editorial writer fired as a retaliatory move.

All of this attention came even as most people in Illinois knew the feds were circling Blagojevich. Months before Blagojevich was charged, few would have blinked if he had been accused of trading appointments or contracts for campaign contributions. *That* investigation—known as Operation Board Games—had been underway for at least four years. It had already nabbed many, including two of Blagojevich's closest advisers and fundraisers. Years earlier, Illinois Attorney General Lisa Madigan had released a letter she received from U.S. Attorney Patrick Fitzgerald citing "very serious allegations of endemic hiring fraud" in the Blagojevich administration. Even though he repeatedly denied it, Blagojevich was long known to be the "Public Official A" identified in a slew of related federal court documents. His campaign fund was known to be under scrutiny.

But what stunned everyone who had been paying attention to these issues was that the new case wasn't about this old conduct (which the feds finally charged years later). If the feds were to be believed, at the time of Blagojevich's December 9, 2008, arrest, his crimes were brand new. They had just happened over the previous seven weeks.

Early on the morning of December 9, FBI Special Agent in Charge Robert Grant knew he had to make the phone call. Grant, who by then had been at the helm of the FBI's Chicago office for four years, didn't want his agents to record it on the tapped line. So he used the state emergency phone that was hooked up to the governor's home.

The phone rang. And it rang. And it rang.

The FBI was worried about some last-minute maneuvering. The night before, agents had learned Blagojevich was booked to appear on *The Early Show* on CBS to discuss the governor's recent support of a local company whose workers had been laid off. A limo was to arrive for the governor just about the time the FBI planned its visit. The FBI then learned that the CBS appearance had been called off at the last minute.

But now, no one was answering the state emergency phone. Grant then tried the governor's cell phone. He believed he woke up Blagojevich with the 6:00 a.m. call.

When the governor answered, Grant told him that federal agents were standing outside his home, and asked him to open the door "so we can do this...quietly" and not attract media attention.

Is this a joke? Blagojevich asked him.

"He wanted to make sure this was an honest call," said Grant, who assured the governor it wasn't a prank. There were numerous charges against him, and they were laid out in a lengthy federal criminal complaint that would be made public that morning, Grant explained.

"He was very cooperative," Grant said, adding that he later told Blagojevich he might want to check on that emergency phone line.

The FBI used protocol in the arrest, and the governor of Illinois was led away from his home in handcuffs.

Across town, early-morning banging on his door woke up the governor's brother, Robert, in the Chicago condo he and his wife had been staying in since he had agreed to come to Chicago from Nashville to help his brother out as head of his campaign fund, Friends of Blagojevich, four months earlier.

The doorbell rang repeatedly. The couple thought it was someone playing around.

They finally opened the door to two FBI agents, who showed their badges and demanded that Rob open his brother's campaign office.

"What if I don't do it?" he asked.

"We'll break the door down," an agent answered.

Blagojevich, a retired Army commander, said he needed to get into some decent clothes. "You look fine," he was told. "Come with us."

He insisted on changing. As he pulled on jeans and a sweater, his wife, Julie, called the governor's wife, Patti, who told her Rod had been arrested.

Rob's stomach dropped.

That same morning, another top law enforcement official was making phone calls.

Patrick Fitzgerald called Rahm Emanuel to alert him that Blagojevich had been arrested—and that there were wiretaps, and that Emanuel was on some of them.

Similar calls were made as a courtesy to a number of people whose names came up on wiretaps, or who were caught on the recordings. Those included Valerie Jarrett, a close friend of Obama's. These people were told that the findings didn't mean they were under scrutiny. In some cases, the feds were reaching out to them that morning as a way to get to them first, perhaps as a way to help secure statements from them. FBI and IRS agents were pounding on doors all across the Chicago area in a synchronized mission, reaching potential witnesses in hopes of getting their words on paper right away.

In Oak Park, political strategist Doug Scofield asked agents to use the back door on their way out. One of his neighbors worked for the *Chicago Tribune*.

As bits and pieces of a 76-page criminal complaint became public, phone lines across the region were lighting up. Lobbyists, politicians, fundraisers, candidates—all were calling their lawyers and trying to decipher the alphabet soup inside the government's charges. There was a lengthy list of unnamed individuals who had interacted with Blagojevich in the preceding months.

As the morning's events unfolded, U.S. Rep. Jesse Jackson Jr. took in the news reports. He heard about allegations involving an unnamed potential Senate candidate. Then he received his phone call. The U.S. Attorney's office was on the other end of the line.

Reporters rushed to the federal courthouse. They paced, waiting for the press conference to begin, reading the criminal complaint aloud. They were stunned. Hardened reporters, who had covered the grittiest of criminal and mob trials, read each other the quotes, marveling at how a governor who already had been so obviously under investigation could have said all of this on tape. And so recently.

Also arrested and charged that morning was John Harris, Blagojevich's chief of staff. The sharp-minded Harris, known for his constant efforts to bring his boss back to reality, was now in his own surreal universe. He was accused of helping his boss corrupt the selection of the next U.S. senator.

The charges Blagojevich and Harris faced spanned three main areas: corrupting the U.S. Senate selection, trying to extort the *Chicago Tribune*, and taking part in schemes to shake down people seeking state business. The charges said Blagojevich ordered that money be held up for Children's Memorial Hospital because he hadn't gotten a campaign contribution. They said he wanted to fire a member of the *Chicago Tribune*'s editorial staff after he was hit with damning editorials. Blagojevich thought he had leverage to get someone fired because the Tribune Company, which at the time owned the Chicago Cubs, wanted state money to revamp Wrigley Field.

Another layer to the complaint involved allegations about Patti Blagojevich. She was depicted as being most un-First-Lady-like. She, too, was dropping f-bombs in wiretapped conversations and was revealed to have sat in on conference calls where her husband discussed getting a benefit in exchange for appointing someone to the U.S. Senate. "Tell them to hold up that fucking Cubs shit!" she was quoted as saying, commenting on what the Tribune Company should and shouldn't get from the state in a pending deal after the newspaper penned blistering editorials about her husband. Patti's foul-mouthed quotes quickly cast her as the Lady Macbeth of the storyline.

It was stuffy inside the eleventh-floor news conference room of the Dirksen Federal Courthouse as journalists waited for Fitzgerald, combing over the papers. TV people shouted over each other, standing on their chairs in the middle of the room to do their live shots. Two television personalities—WBBM's Jay Levine in the left side of the room, WLS's Chuck Goudie over to the right—

were talking over one another as they gave a live update before Fitzgerald walked into the room.

At that point Fitzgerald had been in Chicago for seven years. He'd come to the city while a probe into the administration of a previous governor, George Ryan, was already underway. Ryan was later charged, convicted, and sentenced to six and a half years in prison as a result of that probe, called Operation Safe Road, which led to more than 75 other people being convicted as well. Ryan's petition for residential clemency was just gaining steam, after U.S. Senator Dick Durbin had held a news conference saying Ryan's elderly wife, Lura Lynn Ryan, had sent him a personal appeal on behalf of her husband.

Then Blagojevich was charged.

Fitzgerald didn't exactly come from Mayberry. He arrived at his post as top prosecutor in Chicago after working as an assistant in the Southern District of New York. Besides working on the John Gotti trial in 1998, Fitzgerald's unit indicted nearly two dozen people in connection with two American embassy bombings in Africa that killed two hundred people. Among those indicted— Osama bin Laden.

Still, there's only so much one can prepare for.

Early on in his career in Chicago, Rob Grant had walked into Fitzgerald's office to give him an update on yet another new criminal investigation.

"Is *everything* around here corrupt?" Fitzgerald responded.

Considered one of the country's top prosecutors, Fitzgerald had also been tapped to head a special prosecution into the leak of CIA agent Valerie Plame's identity. Fitzgerald ultimately brought charges against I. Lewis "Scooter" Libby, an aide to Vice President Dick Cheney, which put the prosecutor on the nation's radar screen and made him enemies with the right.

Still, Blagojevich's arrest was something of a defining moment for Fitzgerald.

The news conference was broadcast nationwide, and viewers tuned in, intrigued by the arrest of a sitting governor. It cemented Illinois's reputation as a corrupt state. There was also the Obama factor: the former senator from Illinois was had just made history by becoming the first African-American president, and the Blagojevich news came right on the heels of that story.

When Fitzgerald entered the room, it grew hushed. Journalists were waiting to hear how he would explain the charges—and the handcuffs. What Fitzgerald laid out was a staggering account of how Illinois's chief executive had been handling his office over the preceding two months. Fitzgerald, who was loath to go outside of the "four corners of the indictment," expressed a sense of amazement that was uncharacteristic for him.

"This is a sad day for government. It's a very sad day for Illinois government," Fitzgerald began. "Governor Blagojevich has taken us to a truly new low. Governor Blagojevich has been arrested in the middle of what we can only describe as a political corruption crime spree. We acted to stop that crime spree," he continued to a packed room as shutters repeatedly snapped and video cameras broadcast the remarks live.

"The most cynical behavior in all this, the most appalling, is the fact that Governor Blagojevich tried to sell the appointment to the Senate seat vacated by President-elect Obama," Fitzgerald said.

Then, Fitzgerald uttered a phrase that would be repeated for years and would often come back to haunt the otherwise pristine reputation of the U.S. Attorney: "The conduct," Fitzgerald said, "would make Lincoln roll over in his grave."

Fitzgerald went into specifics, saying he wanted to put the arrest into context. He reminded everyone that it was no secret that a federal investigation into the Blagojevich administration had been going on for years. The Operation Board Games probe was looking at pay-to-play allegations during Blagojevich's tenure, including whether appointments to boards and committees had been traded for political contributions. Further, Blagojevich's friend, fundraiser, and adviser Tony Rezko had been convicted in June of that year, and testimony at Rezko's trial indicated the governor knew about some of the illicit schemes in which Rezko was involved.

As the backdrop of all of that, Fitzgerald explained that the pending Ethics in Government Act was aimed directly at the office of the governor. It would go into effect January 1, 2009, and bar people from contributing to Illinois's chief executive if they were doing business with the state.

"You might have thought in that environment that pay-to-play would slow down," Fitzgerald said. "The opposite happened. It sped up. Government—Blagojevich and others—were working feverishly to get as much money from contractors, shaking them down, pay-to-play, before the end of the year."

Fitzgerald tried to be persuasive in explaining there was an important next step that needed to happen.

"I think this is a moment of truth for Illinois," Fitzgerald said. "In all seriousness, we have times when people decry corruption; and yet, here we have a situation where there appeared to be wide-ranging schemes where people were seeking to make people pay contributions to get contracts or appointments or do other stuff." He repeatedly made it clear that law enforcement needed the public's help.

Though Blagojevich was stuck with his words on tape, investigators needed to decipher who else might have been culpable, Fitzgerald said. It was a giant puzzle, with some pieces coming through the wiretaps. Blagojevich or others could be heard talking about what others did or said. Now the feds had to check out what was true and what wasn't. The remaining pieces needed to be sorted out with live witnesses.

"What we really need is cooperation from people who are not in law enforcement, the people outside who heard or saw things or were approached in ways that felt uncomfortable. If they felt uncomfortable and they think, 'This is not how you run a government,' they ought to come forward and give us that information," Fitzgerald said. "It's very, very important that we get that information, so we can make the right decisions about where to proceed from here."

When Fitzgerald and Grant finished their remarks, the whole room jumped at them at once. Reporters were shouting over each other. What about the timing of the arrest? Blagojevich hadn't appointed anyone yet. He hadn't fired anyone yet. He hadn't taken any money. Further, he was still governor; didn't he still have the power to appoint someone? Didn't he still have time to sign the bills sitting on his desk?

Fitzgerald told everyone not to rush. One at a time. There was no time limit on the news conference. He would stay until all the questions were asked. The arrest happened when it did, Fitzgerald said, because investigators worried about the impact of their inaction down the road. Fitzgerald said he stayed up at night worried someone would get fired from the *Chicago Tribune* if he didn't act. He worried there would be a corrupt appointment of a U.S. senator.

The decision, though, wasn't his alone. The investigative team had huddled and talked it through for weeks, weighing whether to wait or to move when it did.

Fitzgerald said he had resolved not to allow the tainted appointment to go through. There was also reference to a recent leak to the *Chicago Tribune*, which had held off on a story that was published just days earlier at the request of the U.S. Attorney's office. That story addressed the cooperation of longtime Blagojevich friend lobbyist John Wyma and referred to secret recordings of the governor. When Blagojevich read the story, his behavior changed. He canceled a critical meeting with a fundraiser for U.S. Rep. Jesse Jackson Jr., who was believed to have offered more than $1 million to the governor in exchange for a Senate seat appointment. The feds now risked watering down the wiretaps every day they were up after the story ran.

"When we talked about the arrest of Governor Blagojevich, it was a team discussion. We had to talk about what we had, the risk of going to trial, the risk of continuing the Title III [court-approved wiretap] and not arresting," said Grant in an interview. "Everyone agreed that it was the right time and the right thing to do."

Speaking at a news conference the day before his arrest, Blagojevich had invited anyone who wished to tape his conversations. That came up during the media briefing the following day.

"Sir, yesterday, when asking about the taping, the governor said that—he invoked the names 'Nixon' and 'Watergate.' I mean, isn't essentially what the government did here, under the authority of a wiretap court order, the same thing? Didn't FBI agents have to break into the governor's office in order to plant these?"

Fitzgerald didn't hesitate.

"I'm not going to compare FBI agents enforcing the law—trying to stop a senator [sic] from auctioning off a Senate seat, or shutting $8 million out of a children's hospital from being pulled back, or stopping people for greasing the skids to get a bill or get someone fired—with Nixon," Fitzgerald said. "It just—it doesn't fly. What we did was lawful."

Fitzgerald was later blasted for his comments that day. A former U.S. Department of Justice official wrote a letter to national newspapers castigating the U.S Attorney for speaking out of turn.

Defense lawyers had something they could complain about for years—that Fitzgerald had improperly tainted the public's view of the case. Lawyers at the time, though, said Fitzgerald's reaction—one of disbelief combined with disgust—was akin to that of former U.S. Attorney Dan Webb in a news conference about crooked judges in an investigation held decades earlier, known as Operation Greylord. His reaction was the same: he had seen corruption before. This was different. It was an assault against their very system.

On the day of his brother's arrest, Dec. 9, 2008, Rob Blagojevich got into his car, and the FBI followed him to the governor's campaign office on the Northwest Side of the city.

I can't believe this is happening, he thought.

When he arrived at the office, about a dozen FBI agents were there to greet him. He unlocked the door, and they told him to leave. "There's some Cokes in the refrigerator," he told them. "But I expect you to pay for them."

Later that day, he and his wife watched the drama unfold on TV. Rob watched as Fitzgerald accused his brother of taking Illinois to a new low with a political crime spree that would make Abe Lincoln roll over in his grave.

"We sat there in horror, numb and horrified at what had happened," Rob Blagojevich said. "The hyperbole. The incredible exaggeration."

He said he talked back to the TV: "A 'crime spree'? What crime spree?"

Then he heard Fitzgerald say something that dropped like a bomb: "Fundraiser A."

"Oh shit," Rob Blagojevich said aloud. "That's me."

At FBI headquarters, after his arrest and before his appearance in court, the governor had been fingerprinted and had posed for a mug shot. Blagojevich had also been given the option to have a business suit delivered to him to change into before his hearing. Instead, he chose to remain in his jogging outfit. Blagojevich displayed some other odd behavior that would come to exemplify how he acted throughout his ordeal—an unusual combination of incognizance and vanity.

"He was in his running suit. He was stretching, running in place, animated. I couldn't believe it. He couldn't sit still," former FBI supervisor Pete Cullen said. Cullen was in charge of watching over Blagojevich in the time after his arrest. "He kept combing back his hair. It was almost like he was awaiting going on camera."

More than an hour after Fitzgerald's news conference, the Dirksen Federal Courthouse still teemed with reporters, who packed onto benches and into an empty jury box. They looked over the courtroom, trying to find a recognizable defense lawyer. Which high-profile attorney would handle this one? No one looked familiar.

John Harris was seated at a defense table. His lawyer, Terry Ekl, had handled some of the biggest trials in DuPage County.

Where was the governor?

Reporters whispered to each other. He wasn't in the room. Then, in a moment that was surreal to many of those who had spent nearly seven months covering the trial of George Ryan, a side door of the courtroom leading to the prisoner holding area opened.

In came a different governor of Illinois.

Biting his lower lip, the bushy-headed Blagojevich quietly entered the courtroom without a smile. His tracksuit looked awkward in the wood-paneled room crowded with dark business suits. John Harris had also been offered the opportunity to have a suit delivered to him to wear in court. He had chosen to appear in the suit.

The governor sat behind Harris.

"John, good morning," Blagojevich said, shaking his hand.

U.S. Magistrate Judge Nan Nolan handled the hearing that day. The petite woman asked the government to begin.

The lead prosecutor, Reid Schar—a tall, thin man with a shaven head—read the charges. Blagojevich kept his head lowered, hands folded in front of him. At times, he shifted uncomfortably as he listened. Blagojevich looked up at Schar and half rolled his eyes when Schar read portions of the charges involving an attempt to oust members of the *Chicago Tribune*'s editorial board in exchange for giving the Tribune Company state help. But after court, the governor seemed more chipper. He patted Assistant U.S. Attorney Carrie Hamilton on the back and tried joking with her. Two deputy marshals walked over to him and urged him to move along.

The governor called an old family friend that day to serve as his lawyer. The bespectacled Sheldon Sorosky had known the Blagojeviches for some time. He wasn't talking.

Reporters waited for Blagojevich to exit the courthouse, but he was allowed to leave through a secure entrance. He was still a sitting politician, and with the governorship came a perk—he had his own security team from the Illinois State Police. In an increasingly volatile political climate, officials with the state police were among the few whom Blagojevich still trusted. On the day of his arrest, court security deferred to the governor's detail and allowed a backdoor departure from the building. Blagojevich made no public statements. He rode out of the courthouse's basement in the backseat of a car driven by the state police. A *Sun-Times* photographer was in the right spot to get a shot of the solemn-faced governor. Blagojevich was sunken in the backseat of the car, next to a window. That photo covered the entirety of the newspaper's front page the next day. The headline: "*Shame.*"

Chapter Two

Wired

It was October of 2002, and the Republican candidate for governor, Jim Ryan, was so angry that he began shouting.

"The voters of Illinois should be very worried about a guy who would sink to these depths to win an election," Ryan screamed to an audience watching the debate. "If they want him, they can have him!"

Ryan had just endured a blistering exchange at a gubernatorial debate with Rod Blagojevich. The race was wide open after the GOP incumbent, a different Ryan—George Ryan—announced he would not run for reelection, as his administration was being probed for corruption by federal investigators.

Blagojevich, who had handily raised $7.5 million in the first six months of that year, easily outpacing Jim Ryan, had just pricked an open sore that was the most sensitive of political scandals in Illinois: the deaths of six children in a fiery crash caused by an unlicensed trucker.

"Have you no shame, Rod?" Ryan implored. "Have you no shame?...You're not going to say that. And I'm not going to let you get away with it, not with my family sitting there, because that is an absolute shameful thing to say."

That trucker, who could not speak English, had paid a bribe to get his commercial driver's license. He hadn't understood radioed warnings from other truckers telling him that his mud flap assembly was dangling off his truck. The piece fell off and hit the gas tank of a minivan driven by Chicago minister Scott Willis and his wife. The van exploded in a fiery crash, and the six Willis children aboard all died. The crash had happened in 1994, while George Ryan was still Illinois Secretary of State. But aggressive prosecutors and FBI agents pushed and pushed, as did Illinois State Police, and eventually linked that driver's bribe to cash that flowed into George Ryan's campaign fund. And they later found evidence that Ryan had covered up the investigation into the crash.

Now, with the gubernatorial election weeks away, Blagojevich was attempting to link the tragedy to his opponent. Blagojevich, a former boxer, must have known that the Willis charge was hitting below the belt. He likely brought it up to play on Jim Ryan's biggest weakness: that he had the same last name as George Ryan even though the two had no familial relation.

"On Election Day 1994, two things happened. Both Ryans—George and Jim—got elected, and a tragic accident occurred," Blagojevich said during the debate. "Neither George Ryan nor Jim Ryan did anything to change that failed system and, as every day passed, the corruption continued."

Jim Ryan was still seething after the debate. Some of his words at the time were strikingly similar to those used by Fitzgerald years later.

"Politics has reached a new low in Illinois," Ryan said. "I cannot believe that this guy will stoop to this level to get elected governor. Anyone who will do that should not be elected governor."

Blagojevich later backed off his incendiary remarks. But he kept up his aggressive campaigning to the end, continuing to outraise Jim Ryan along the way. In November 2002, Blagojevich was elected to his first term as governor. As his power grew, so did that of the people he empowered in his administration, including fundraisers Tony Rezko and Chris Kelly. For his chief of staff, Blagojevich tapped his old roommate, Lon Monk.

There were some other key appointments Blagojevich made early in his tenure. These included the reappointment of wealthy North Shore fundraiser Stuart Levine—a major contributor to Jim Ryan—to two state boards. Then, in the spring of 2003, Blagojevich selected Larry Trent to head the Illinois State Police.

It was a move that Blagojevich would later openly regret. In October 2008, the Illinois State Police, which has responsibility for protecting the governor, received a request from Rod Blagojevich's people: to do a sweep for bugs at Blagojevich's campaign office. The state police agreed to do it even though, as a political office, it was outside of their jurisdiction. A special technician with the agency visited the North Side office to carry out the orders. After spending some time inside, he gave the Blagojevich people a thumbs-up, signaling he had found no recording devices inside.

But the bugs were, in fact, in place. The state police employee even knew where they were. He just pretended not to detect them. And that let the FBI listen in. Free and clear.

The FBI's surveillance of the governor of Illinois did not unfold in the most orthodox way. Blagojevich's people had asked for the bug sweep just before what investigators believed would be a critical October 22, 2008, meeting inside the campaign finance office between Blagojevich and his inner circle.

The request rankled the upper echelon of the Illinois State Police. It was widely known that Blagojevich was under investigation. Now, not only was the governor asking the agency to use state resources for his political campaign office, but the request, if carried out, could end up obstructing justice. Illinois State Police Deputy Director Charles Brueggemann called Rob Grant at the FBI to tell him what was going on.

"Out of blue we got a phone call...saying, 'Hey, we got a really weird request.' Why would you do a sweep for mics? What are you protecting against?" Grant said federal officials asked themselves at the time. "So we had an unusual sweep request that wasn't in a government facility, and we had other information, and when you put the two together it was 'a-ha.' It set off an alarm."

The FBI and the U.S. Attorney's office knew they had to act fast. To get a judge to agree to allow bugs, the government had to show first that there was no other way to get the needed information. They felt there wasn't. Though it appeared Blagojevich was fearing listening devices were in place, they weren't yet. His administration's interest on that specific date, however, raised the FBI's suspicion to the point that they knew they wanted to be in place listening. It was just days earlier that a longtime friend of Blagojevich had approached them with his lawyer, Zach Fardon, who also happened to be an ex-federal prosecutor who worked the George Ryan case. John Wyma, once chief of staff to Blagojevich when he was in Congress, had been hit with a subpoena. Wyma was ready to talk. Investigators asked him to wear a wire. He refused.

Wyma had helped the feds fulfill a critical legal obligation. They had to give the judge evidence that criminal wrongdoing was going on at present, not just in the past. Earlier that October, Wyma had told officials the governor was racing to raise more than $2 million in cash before a new ethics law went into effect the next January 1. Wyma said Blagojevich was shaking down people who were doing business with the state.

"If they don't perform, fuck them," Blagojevich threatened, according to Wyma. Now, Wyma was telling the feds about a fundraising strategy session to be held at the governor's campaign office.

The lead agent on the case, FBI Special Agent Daniel Cain, said Wyma's cooperation helped bring the case to the next level.

"It was critical that we were able to file the affidavit with information that convinced a judge that there was sufficient probable cause in order to install the microphones and have the wiretaps," Cain said in a public interview with an internal FBI online broadcast. "This allowed agents to surreptitiously listen and record conversations that could serve as evidence of fraud and extortion."

Setting up mics against any target, no less a sitting governor, typically involved extensive planning. In this case, however, they had just less than 48 hours to execute, Grant said. The U.S. Attorney's office and the FBI worked on separate tracks. First, they had to get legal clearance from a judge to put in the bugs. Next, the FBI had to use its special operations team to install the devices, a task that is among the most delicate of operations inside the bureau.

The agent from a special operations team had to get past different walls of security to break into the campaign offices without notice. He didn't sleep for 36 hours straight. But he pulled it off. Two mics were put into the office—and they both worked.

"You're installing things with duct tape and gum and Band-Aids," Grant said of the typical difficulties of pulling off such a feat. "That was the key to everything else that followed and led to the arrest." (Later, Fitzgerald would buy that agent a pricey bottle of vodka as a thank-you.)

But it was the tip from the Illinois State Police that hastened one of the most sensitive bug installations in the state's history. Both Trent and Brueggemann secretly kept in contact with the FBI throughout the final months of 2008. Brueggemann's phone records, obtained by the *Sun-Times* in 2011, show a flurry of phone calls back and forth with the FBI and Grant before and after several of the critical dates in the timeline that led to Blagojevich's arrest. Brueggemann sometimes followed the talks with calls to Trent's home phone.

From October 17 to 24, Brueggemann's phone records showed 16 calls to or from the FBI. On the eve of the December 9, 2008, arrest, Brueggemann talked to the FBI for at least 35 minutes, the records showed. The state police were asked to sweep the campaign office that day. That was three days after a *Chicago Tribune* article revealed the feds were listening in on Blagojevich. The records also show five calls between the two agencies on December 30, 2008, the day Blagojevich appointed Roland Burris, former Illinois attorney general, to the U.S. Senate seat.

"I have no regrets about our responsibility to the people of Illinois and our responsibility to justice," Trent said. "The balancing act of maintaining profound confidentiality while performing certain duties presented unique and difficult challenges. I believe we simply did our job as the public should expect us to do." Trent stepped down from his post in 2009 and took a job for the U.S. Department of Homeland Security. Brueggemann, now in the private sector, said, "The state police did the right thing."

The revelation that the same agency that protected the governor took part in his downfall appeared to stun Rod and Patti Blagojevich during a 2011 *Sun-Times* interview. "Wow," Rod said, describing his state police security detail as "quasi-family." The detail that worked the closest with the family, including the visible presence in front of the governor's Ravenswood Manor home, was largely kept in the dark about the agency's work with the FBI.

In an interview, Blagojevich said he regretted naming Trent to his position, saying he had thought about putting Tom Dart in the post instead. Dart, a former state lawmaker, went on to be a popular Cook County Sheriff.

In the interview, Blagojevich distanced himself from the request for the bug sweeps, saying he didn't order them himself, and adding, "They were routine."

Patti Blagojevich said "it was sad" when Pat Quinn, who succeeded her husband as Illinois governor, pulled the security detail right after the Illinois General Assembly impeached her husband.

"They had tears in their eyes," she said, explaining that at the time there was a media horde planted in their front yard. "It was like they were leaving us to not being able to leave our front door to get the kids to school."

That initial bug installation propelled the investigation, giving authorities evidence to ask a judge for expanded wiretaps of phone lines. Most of the recorded conversations came from a wiretap on the phone in Blagojevich's home. By 2008, most people knew that he was spending more and more time at his house on Chicago's Northwest Side. It was obvious he was growing increasingly frustrated in Springfield, having butted heads for years with Illinois House Speaker Michael Madigan and other lawmakers. The Blagojevich administration had experienced little success advancing his causes there. Then, in early 2008, a number of state politicians accused him of handing out the deepest budget cuts to his enemies.

"I don't think there's any question it was done in a petty and vindictive manner," said then-Lieutenant Governor Pat Quinn. Quinn himself lost 17 percent from his budget after leading efforts to give voters the chance to recall Blagojevich—efforts that came long before Blagojevich was criminally charged. "I think every press conference I had on recall cost me another percentage point."

After Madigan stymied Blagojevich's legislative agenda that year, Blagojevich cut the budget of the House Speaker's daughter, Illinois Attorney General Lisa Madigan, by 25 percent. The governor cut his own bottom line by just 3 percent that year.

But there was far more serious trouble for Blagojevich than mere political squabbles. After months of rumors that the feds were closing in on some of the governor's top people, Rezko was indicted in October 2006. The charges didn't bode well for Blagojevich. The allegations involved conduct affecting Blagojevich's administration, and the feds were making it increasingly clear that the person who kept giving Rezko more and more power over contracts and state and board appointments was the governor himself.

The route to Rezko had been as significant as it was circuitous. Not long after Blagojevich took office in his first term as governor, a woman named Pam Davis, the president and CEO of Edward Hospital in Naperville, Illinois, was pitching plans to a state board for an expansion in nearby Plainfield. In 2003, as she sought approval, she said people began to strong-arm her into using a contractor and a politically connected financing firm that had no experience building hospitals. If she did as she was told, then the new hospital would get the needed nod from the little-known Illinois Health Facilities Planning Board—a panel that included gubernatorial appointees. There was a particular key individual who sat on that board: Stuart Levine.

Davis chose not to play. She went to the FBI and cooperated with their investigation. At one point, Davis wore a wire in her bra. As the probe gained steam and the subpoenas began flying, one thing became clear to investigators: Levine was someone to watch. Once Levine's phones were tapped, he was revealed to be one of the most crooked individuals investigators had ever seen. In some of the tapes, he was heard discussing how he controlled votes on the hospital board, at times with Rezko's direction, as a way to line up kickbacks.

The recordings revealed Levine to be a cunning con man who ripped people off for sport. The victims included a friend who trusted Levine enough to make him executor of his estate. Levine ended up stealing $1 million from the dead man's estate even though he admitted he already had been generously compensated for his work.

One day in 2004, agents approached Levine. They played tapes of him talking to insiders, scheming to take kickbacks and to fix votes on state boards. It was beyond jarring to the man once worth $70 million. Levine, who lived on gorgeous lakefront property in Highland Park, had much to fear and a great deal to lose. The married father of two kids was well respected and had money tied up in deals throughout the state.

But there was something else: the buttoned-down, bespectacled Levine, who was often linked to more conservative political stands, led a double life. It was so secret, his best friends didn't know about it. Neither did his family. For years, Levine frequented a sketchy place in north suburban Chicago called the Purple Hotel. The hotel's exterior was, indeed, purple. There, he met with other men for all-night drug binges. Levine, by his own admission, snorted crystal meth and cocaine.

"I'd prepare them in lines a half-inch long and very, very narrow," Levine testified at Rezko's trial, adding that he paid for all the drugs at the parties, spending about $1,000 per party. "I would stay out all night," he said. He hid his behavior "in order to deceive my family."

At one point in 2008, a filing briefly made public in the Rezko case revealed that Levine had frequented male prostitutes. It was a point that Rezko's defense unsuccessfully tried to raise before jurors, arguing that Levine was carrying around an explosive secret that blew up when confronted by the FBI. As such, he had incredible motivation to make up stories about Rezko out of fear his other life would become known.

With so much to hide in his personal life, it would surprise few to hear that Levine agreed to cooperate after the FBI approached him. Levine not only started spilling everything he knew, but he too agreed to wear a wire while talking to other figures of interest to investigators. These included a notorious political insider named Ed Vrdolyak—a powerful, slick former alderman who'd made millions in his career as a lawyer. He also knew how to make a deal. He was nicknamed "Fast Eddie" because he always seemed on the edge of questionable deals, but just out of investigators' reach. Levine ended up snaring Vrdolyak by catching him on a wire discussing how to split a kickback on a real estate deal.

Vrdolyak was only the beginning. Another person caught on tape was William Cellini, a Downstate businessman known for securing hundreds of millions of dollars in state contracts over the years. Cellini was known as a power broker who knew how to pull the strings behind the scenes. Since Levine's crimes were extensive, so too was his knowledge of who else had their hands in the cookie jar. Over the course of hundreds of secret sessions with investigators, Levine exposed the dirty underbelly of Illinois politics, strengthening the government's investigation of Blagojevich's administration. In addition to his discussions with the feds, hundreds of Levine's telephone conversations were recorded. Now Levine was agreeing to walk authorities through the recorded phone calls, to be the narrator and explain the context of what everything meant.

And thus began Operation Board Games. The federal probe took a serious look at the work of two boards on which Levine sat, the Illinois Health Facilities Planning Board and the Teachers' Retirement System (TRS) board. One of the most explosive charges leveled against Rezko was not backed up by tapes. Levine told authorities he'd had a significant meeting with Rezko at the Standard Club in Chicago to discuss corrupt dealings. There, Levine said, the two had talked about how Rezko agreed to $3.9 million as his share from a series of illicit kickbacks. The specific dollar amount was scribbled on a napkin during their meeting at the club, he said.

"I told Mr. Rezko that there was an opportunity for a lot of money to be made," Levine said. "I wanted Mr. Rezko to understand the magnitude of what could be done with these companies." Rezko later called Levine's testimony on this point a complete fabrication. At Rezko's trial, prosecutors couldn't give much evidence to support that claim. They did show a receipt from that night and played tapes on which Levine is heard making arrangements to meet with Rezko.

Rezko was ultimately convicted in June 2008 at a trial where Blagojevich's name came up repeatedly, including on tape, where he was called "the Big Guy." Previously, prosecutors had a different way of describing him. Blagojevich had long been known as "Public Official A" in court documents drawn up by federal prosecutors, even though he denied being the person to whom this referred each time he was asked by reporters. Just before Rezko's trial, however, U.S. District Judge Amy St. Eve issued a lengthy ruling, and in it she confirmed that Blagojevich was indeed Public Official A.

Later in 2008, Cellini was indicted on charges that stemmed from Levine tapes. Cellini was accused of trying to shake down Hollywood producer Thomas Rosenberg for $1.5 million that would go to Blagojevich's campaign fund. The charges said Rosenberg was told to ante up if he wanted his investment fund to continue receiving lucrative contributions from the TRS.

It was in this climate that Blagojevich, increasingly struggling to raise campaign cash, began to hole up in his home. The allegations piling up around him made it nearly impossible for him to tap anyone for campaign money. He saw his fundraising abilities slipping away with his political power. The conversations he was having with his aides seemed to bear out these frustrations. That was what federal authorities were interested in.

FBI Special Agent Dan Cain eventually said that his office captured crooked talk on 10 different phones or places in the course of the probe. The result was more than 5,000 recordings of the former governor, top aides, and some of the most powerful people in state and national politics.

Chapter Three

Shame to Fame

After the governor's arrest, a dark cloud settled over the Blagojevich house, squeezing out the life and din that usually filled the place. The governor wasn't talking. He and Patti weren't even leaving their home. Deb Mell, Patti's sister and also a state representative, was seen bringing groceries to the door. Reporters were always stationed outside, despite the frigid weather. Blagojevich had become a pariah, the center of an ugly scandal that was talked about from Chicago to Washington, D.C.

It was as if there had been a death in the family of this once-bright political star. Six years earlier, Blagojevich had been elected to his first term as governor. He was only the fourth Democrat since 1940 to hold that office. The late political columnist Steve Neal wrote in 2002 that "Rod Blagojevich shouldn't be underestimated. As the state's first Democratic governor in three decades, Blagojevich brings a new style and formidable political skills to the job. His election is good for Chicago. He will become the first Chicagoan in a dozen years to live in the governor's mansion and will be responsive to the city's needs. His election assures the future of O'Hare expansion."

Blagojevich never did live in the governor's mansion. He wanted to stay in Chicago to keep his daughters in school with their friends. It was a decision that rankled Downstate voters. It was also a decision that kept him within the reach of one Patrick Fitzgerald.

Then–*Sun-Times* political reporter Scott Fornek noted in an early campaign story that Blagojevich had been rolling in campaign money early on, mentioning the $7.5 million he had raised in the first six months of 2002. "Democrat Rod Blagojevich raised more money this year than any Democrat or Republican in the last two gubernatorial elections at this point in the campaign," Fornek wrote.

Six years later, the circumstances could not have been more different. Blagojevich couldn't find people willing to make donations and have their names connected to his tainted administration. Authorities would later say he grew desperate for cash, causing him to make repeated, unguarded demands for money. If there was a low point for the governor in his battle with his legal case, it may have been in December 2008. *Sun-Times* photographer John White captured Blagojevich making a break from his house one day. Blagojevich was trying to avoid cameras, and, in the photo, he lurched forward beside a sign commonly posted in Chicago alleyways. It read: "Warning. Target: Rats." After the paper published the photo, the sign mysteriously disappeared from that alley.

It was around this time that Blagojevich paid a visit to Ed Genson, a legendary defense lawyer. Blagojevich was pondering his options, including whether he should resign. Rumors swirled as the public wondered what path he'd take. On December 19, a Friday, Blagojevich was to hold a news conference to make his position clear. It was the most anticipated news event in Chicago since Fitzgerald had announced the charges.

When Blagojevich walked out into the firestorm of media, something was evident: he had shed the shame from his face. He launched into his remarks.

"I will fight. I will fight. I will fight until I take my last breath," Blagojevich said, seeming to pour himself into the statement. "I have done nothing wrong. I'm not going to quit a job the people hired me to do because of false accusations and a political lynch mob."

Like the Chicago Golden Gloves boxer he'd been in his youth, Blagojevich conjured the image of a fighter. In his first campaign for governor in 2002, Blagojevich and his aides would sum up each day's success in boxing terms: 10-10 for a draw, 10-9 a win, 10-8 a decisive win, a knockdown, and so on. Once he took office, he didn't shy away from picking political fights, even with some of the most powerful politicians in the state. Those included his father-in-law, Chicago Alderman Dick Mell, as well as Michael Madigan.

"Now I know there are some powerful forces arrayed against me," Blagojevich said that day. "It's kind of lonely right now. But I have on my side the most powerful ally there is, and it's the truth. And besides, I have the personal knowledge that I have not done anything wrong. Let me tell you what I'm not going to do. I'm not going to do what my accusers and political enemies have been doing, and that is talk about this case in 30-second sound bites on *Meet the Press* or on the TV news. Now, I'm dying to answer these charges. I am dying to show you how innocent I am. And I want to assure everyone who's here and everyone who's listening that I intend to answer every allegation that comes my way. However, I intend to answer them in the appropriate forum—in a court of law."

He included a recitation of a portion of Rudyard Kipling's poem "If," the first several lines of which go like this:

> If you can keep your head when all about you
> Are losing theirs and blaming it on you,
> If you can trust yourself when all men doubt you,
> But make allowance for their doubting too...

In all, he talked for just three minutes and took no questions.

Two of his lawyers then stepped up to the microphones—Sam Adam Jr. and Sheldon Sorosky. With reporters shouting out portions of the criminal complaint, the two attorneys said it was difficult for the governor to defend himself. By then, they knew how long the FBI had been recording the governor, but they had only seen "snippets" of the evidence.

Fighting to defend himself clearly felt good to Blagojevich. It suited him. He grew undeterred.

Across town, on that very day, federal authorities were taking some of the most sensitive interviews of the investigation. Valerie Jarrett, whom Obama had recently picked to be a White House adviser, was sitting down with FBI agents and federal prosecutors. Agents talked to Jarrett at her Hubbard Street office.

When Blagojevich is repeatedly heard on secret recordings trying to craft a deal in exchange for appointing Jarrett to the Senate seat, he's often talking about wanting an appointment to the president's cabinet, as well. Blagojevich liked to call himself the "healthcare governor," having put in place the All Kids program, which aimed to bring healthcare to every child in Illinois. In Blagojevich's mind, that meant he was qualified to head Health and Human Services for the Obama administration. Jarrett said she laughed when she first heard the idea. It was absurd for Blagojevich to think he could get a cabinet appointment, as a guy who had been pounded by negative headlines for years.

Jarrett had, however, entertained the possibility of becoming the U.S. senator, something that people close to her had told her she should pursue. The first person to bring it up had been the state's senior senator, Dick Durbin, who also happened to be the second most powerful Democrat in the chamber. Durbin had planted the notion earlier that year, saying Jarrett would be an optimal candidate and that he'd enjoy campaigning with her. Jarrett took it to heart enough that she raised the issue with her family.

Obama, though, had worked to dissuade her. He stressed the political realities. It would mean intense campaigning and fundraising. Obama thought she would get more out of being in the White House. Michelle Obama later echoed that sentiment, telling Jarrett that she, too, wanted Jarrett in the White House.

But the White House was getting crowded. Namely, Jarrett thought Obama was making a mistake by asking Rahm Emanuel to be his chief of staff. Jarrett tried to convince Obama that the ever-intense Emanuel would be in direct conflict with Obama's "no drama" policy. As the presidential election neared, Jarrett began to hear support from one of the most powerful unions in the country—the Service Employees International Union (SEIU). As the former chairman of the Chicago Transit Authority, Jarrett had worked with the union and had a good relationship with it.

On November 4, 2008—Election Day—Jarrett traveled to Indianapolis with Obama. When she returned she heard from Tom Balanoff, who headed SEIU's Illinois chapter. Balanoff told her he would approach Blagojevich about Jarrett and the Senate seat.

The day before sitting down with Jarrett, federal authorities conducted an even more sensitive interview: they questioned Barack Obama at his transition office. It was perhaps the first time a president-elect was interviewed by the FBI between his election and inauguration. There was a considerable political distance between Obama and Blagojevich. Obama had stayed away from the governor, but especially so in recent months. There was, however, one powerful connection between them—Tony Rezko. Obama and Rezko had been close for years, and Rezko was a notable fundraiser for Obama. Obama had said that Rezko raised as much as $60,000 for him during his political career.

In June 2005, in a move that would later haunt Obama as he sought higher office, Obama and Rezko's wife, Rita, purchased adjoining real estate in Chicago's Kenwood neighborhood. Obama paid $1.65 million for a Georgian revival mansion, while Rezko paid $625,000 for the adjacent undeveloped lot. Both closed on their properties on the same day. The transaction occurred at a time when it was widely known that Rezko was under investigation, and while other Illinois politicians were distancing themselves from him. Obama later called his decision to buy the property "boneheaded." After Rezko was indicted on federal charges in 2006, Obama donated $11,500 to charity. That total represented what Rezko had contributed to the senator's federal campaign fund.

In yet another sensitive interview, the feds talked to Rahm Emanuel not long after he accepted the chief of staff position at the White House. Accepting this position meant he had to give up his seat in the U.S. House of Representatives. Though Blagojevich had become a political pariah by 2008, it was clear from their interviews that Obama, Jarrett, and Emanuel had all been willing to deal with him in private or through intermediaries. Blagojevich, after all, still held power, and Emanuel thought it could go beyond the Senate seat.

Four days after the presidential election, Emanuel told Blagojevich he wanted local politician Forrest Claypool to fill his position in Congress, explaining he wanted "somebody there, you know, that doesn't want to make it a lifetime commitment." Though Emanuel was going to the White House, he was interested in possibly returning to his House seat with an eye toward eventually becoming Speaker. Emanuel said that Claypool would only stay in Congress for a couple of years. "And then he wants to go to the cabinet," Emanuel told Blagojevich. Blagojevich repeatedly told Emanuel he couldn't appoint someone to the post. It had to be a special election.

But Emanuel pressed him.

"You would appoint somebody to finish those three weeks," Emanuel said, if he were to leave his position early. "And then he, and then he gets, you know, all we are giving him is three weeks of a head start...It's not like Forrest doesn't have a name or anything like that. It gives him a head start and a presumption." Emanuel said he had his legal people looking into it. At the end of that particular excerpt of the call, Emanuel told Blagojevich, "I will not forget this...I appreciate it. That's all I am going to say. I don't want to go, you and I shouldn't go farther." Ultimately, Blagojevich could not, in fact, legally appoint someone to Emanuel's seat.

It was a frigid winter day in January 2008. Tony Rezko was asleep in the comfort of his Wilmette, Illinois, mansion bedroom when federal agents came to the door and told him he was under arrest.

Rezko was puzzled. He had already been charged by authorities long before; his trial date was in a matter of weeks. In fact, Rezko had been overseas when the charges first came down, and he returned to the United States regardless, providing authorities with his flight number and directions for picking him up at O'Hare Airport. Now he was under arrest, with authorities claiming he was a flight risk.

As agents took away her husband, Rita Rezko yelled out to them, "Your wives are whores!"

From his palatial home, once graced by high-end attendees including foreign dignitaries and top state officials, Rezko was now on his way to the federal lockup downtown. At the MCC, or the Metropolitan Correctional Center, Rezko was immediately placed in solitary confinement.

"The only thing I thought of: it was cold in the hole. It was January 28. They didn't give me a blanket," Rezko said in a 2012 interview with the *Sun-Times*. "I was shivering. I was cold."

Rezko believed the feds were trying to break him, to make him take a plea and flip on Blagojevich before his trial, which was to begin the following month.

"I believe it was by design," Rezko said of his arrest.

Rezko was soon just another prisoner, being moved to and from court in shackles. Sometimes, on his way to the courthouse, he would see a fellow prisoner he recognized.

Once, he passed a notorious Chicago mafia boss, Joey "the Clown" Lombardo. Now elderly, Lombardo had been part of the landmark 2007 "Family Secrets" mob trial. He was charged with wide-reaching mob activity and eventually convicted for the murder of government witness Daniel Seifert, who had been gunned down in 1974 just yards from his wife and four-year-old son. Lombardo was in the jail's general population, not in solitary confinement.

"I questioned, why was a person like that in the general population?" Rezko said. "They won't allow me to be in the general population?"

Rezko knew he had crossed the legal line in his dealings with Blagojevich. Some of what the newspapers had reported was true: so-called pay-to-play was happening under the governor. By Rezko's account, he and Blagojevich would have conversations about who to place on what state board or committee. The influencing factor was the level of campaign contribution the person had made to Blagojevich, Rezko said.

"We would have the discussions. X, Y, and Z made a $50,000 [contribution] and looking to be placed on a board, where should we place that person if that person specifically requested to be placed on board. Yeah. We had these discussions," Rezko said.

Rezko insisted, though, that Levine made up the story about the two of them splitting millions of dollars in kickbacks from state deals. Rezko was resolved on going to trial. Levine spent parts of 15 days on the witness stand under cross-examination by Rezko's attorney, Joseph Duffy.

When Rezko was eventually convicted in June 2008, he had a change of heart about talking to the feds. From the MCC, he was taken to secret meetings with federal agents and prosecutors where he began giving them information about Blagojevich and others. During that time, Blagojevich himself was arrested—something that stunned even Rezko, who couldn't believe Blagojevich actually said everything he was caught saying on tape.

"I thought he knew better, I should say. I was surprised. I was surprised that he had said the things he said with regard to the Senate seat on the phone," Rezko stated. "I wasn't surprised that these conversations take place, I was surprised that these conversations take place on the phone."

After Blagojevich was charged, Rezko's importance to the feds diminished. He had nothing to do with the highest-profile part of the Blagojevich case, which involved Obama's Senate seat. Rezko was already behind bars when the seat was vacated. Rezko did, however, give authorities some potentially valuable nuggets. These included the fact that he once relayed a bribe offer to Obama, who refused it, according to documents accidentally made public in the course of Blagojevich's federal case.

Rezko did draw other connections for the feds. But from the beginning, authorities were worried about him.

He seemed to be holding back.

For his part, Obama said he was removed from any talks concerning his successor in the Senate.

"The president-elect had no contact or communication with Governor Blagojevich or members of his staff about the Senate seat. In various conversations with transition staff and others, the president-elect expressed his preference that Valerie Jarrett work with him in the White House," Counsel Greg Craig said in a report commissioned by Obama after he was elected. The report was released in December 2008, to deal with a headache Obama definitely didn't need as he was nearing his inauguration. "He also stated that he would neither stand in her way if she wanted to pursue the Senate seat nor actively seek to have her or any other particular candidate appointed to the vacancy," the report said. It didn't mention one fact, however.

The night before his historic election to the presidency, Obama personally dialed up union leader Tom Balanoff. According to Balanoff, Obama gave him the green light to talk to Blagojevich about appointing Jarrett to the Senate.

Meanwhile, in the state's capitol, an impeachment panel was mobilizing against Blagojevich. The person behind the effort was Michael Madigan.

The two men couldn't have been more different. Madigan had amassed power over three decades as House Speaker. He was serious, measured, and precise. Blagojevich, by contrast, was chronically late and known to renege on promises. He tended to govern more like he was still running his campaign, with a focus on big ideas and sound bites.

The two had battled for years over the state's budget, among other issues. Blagojevich was criticized for holding news conferences and blaming lawmakers for a stalemate in the General Assembly, which resulted in plummeting public opinion regarding the governor. Blagojevich had few allies, aside from Illinois Senate President Emil Jones, and had no hope of seeing his initiatives become law. So just six days after Blagojevich's arrest, Madigan didn't hesitate to step forward and help lead the House to begin impeachment proceedings.

"I treat today's action as a very significant governmental action of the gravest consideration," said Madigan after the vote. A 21-member panel, comprising 12 Democrats and 9 Republicans, was to decide whether to recommend impeachment to the full House. There was nothing in the Illinois state constitution that defined an impeachable offense. But Madigan said the action was designed to address Blagojevich's "abuse of power," and that the governor's constitutional rights to due process and equal protection would be guaranteed. Madigan vowed to reach out to Fitzgerald as part of the impeachment effort.

Meanwhile, Blagojevich was burrowing in. He signed horseracing legislation that his criminal charges identified as having been held up by the governor because he hadn't received a particular campaign contribution. The bill would divert proceeds from the state's four top-grossing casinos to racetracks as a way to salvage the state's dying horseracing industry.

It was around this time that Blagojevich did something that would forever define his legal battle: he met up with one Glenn Selig, a publicist from Florida and a former TV reporter. Selig was known for handling the media for another well-known defendant hailing from Illinois, suspected wife murderer Drew Peterson.

Blagojevich hired Selig after his arrest.

"When you see someone being arrested, you automatically think: What did they do? You don't think: I wonder if they did anything," Selig said. As the impeachment moved to the Illinois Senate for trial, Selig went full throttle with Blagojevich's media efforts. The governor announced he had no plans to show up for the impeachment trial. Instead, he was scheduling appearances on a series of national television shows, including ABC's *Good Morning America* and *The View* and CNN's *Larry King Live*.

Not long after those appearances were announced, Ed Genson did the unthinkable. He quit Blagojevich's criminal case. Genson said Blagojevich should not have launched a media blitz. But it was also clear that Genson was sparring behind the scenes with other lawyers on the case. Blagojevich didn't relent. He moved forward with his national media tour and refused to talk to local media, particularly steering clear of print interviews. More and more frequently, when an Illinois resident turned on the TV at night, Blagojevich would be sitting down with one host or another, talking about how he was innocent.

"Everyone thought he was off of his rocker. Everyone thought I was off my rocker. They thought we were nuts," Selig said. "You have to ignore those comments, obviously, because when you've been maligned as he was, you have two choices: you either accept that…or you fight."

Chapter Four

The Congressman

Early on December 9, 2008, the day of the governor's arrest, the feds also paid a visit to Raghuveer Nayak at his in Oak Brook, Illinois, home. Nayak was a wealthy member of the Indian community in Chicago and also happened to be close to Jesse Jackson Jr. and his political machine. Nayak told authorities that Jesse Jackson Jr. hadn't authorized him to do anything improper. There was no quid pro quo with the Senate seat, he told agents.

Later that same day, Nayak was picking up his son from school when he got a phone call from an aide to the Reverend Jesse Jackson. The Reverend wanted Nayak to call right away.

Jesse Jackson Jr. was one of the state's biggest political rising stars. Well-spoken, good-looking, and the son of a celebrated activist who had grown up to make his own name for himself, Jackson was on a trajectory upward. With the U.S. Senate's only African-American member likely headed to the presidency, he felt he was the best person to take over that position for the state of Illinois.

As Blagojevich weighed whom to appoint, Jackson won the endorsement of the *Sun-Times*. Some early public-opinion polling had Jackson's camp feeling confident, despite the fact that his relationship with Blagojevich was strained. Still, Jackson pushed hard to meet with the governor. He met with friends of Blagojevich. He reached out to Balanoff, asking him to help broker a meeting with the governor. He met with John Wyma to see if he could lend some advice. Finally, on December 8, 2008, Blagojevich granted Jackson a meeting. The two spoke for 90 minutes, during which Jackson apologized for reneging on a promise to endorse Blagojevich in a gubernatorial primary race that had included former Illinois Attorney General Roland Burris as an opponent. As it turned out, this meeting with Jackson was not recorded because it took place in a State government office downtown that was not bugged.

After the meeting with Jackson, Blagojevich headed off to a small fundraiser thrown by attorney Gery Chico, a former top aide to Mayor Daley and one-time president of the Chicago Park District board. For his part, Jackson was flying high. He told close friends he thought it went well. Blagojevich seemed in good spirits, too.

"When the governor came out, he looked pretty happy," said one source.

The very next morning, Blagojevich was arrested. He was hit with pay-to-play allegations, but the most explosive allegation held that a Senate hopeful had promised, through an "emissary," campaign cash in exchange for the Senate seat appointment. The criminal complaint disclosed that Blagojevich and his brother discussed picking "Senate Candidate 5" over other candidates because of the emissary's promise to raise money for the governor's cash-strapped campaign fund.

Meanwhile, Jackson was in a panic. People were calling him, citing portions of the criminal complaint. Was he Senate Candidate 5? Had he—or someone on his behalf—made an offer of $1 million and another $500,000 in exchange for the Senate seat appointment? The feds had Blagojevich on tape referring to this. It had escaped no one that the governor's arrest came immediately after Blagojevich's meeting with Jackson, leaving a presumption that the feds had moved specifically to prevent Blagojevich from appointing Jackson.

"I'm somewhere between a nervous breakdown and insanity," Jackson said over the phone. He was talking to David Glockner of the U.S. Attorney's office, according to sources familiar with the exchange. Glockner, chief of the office's criminal section, is a fixture in the prosecutor's office in Chicago. Jackson had spoken to the office before, on his own terms. Earlier that same year, he had phoned Glockner to talk about some allegations involving Blagojevich. Jackson said he believed Blagojevich had refused to appoint his wife, Sandi Jackson, to a position with the Illinois Lottery years earlier because Jackson didn't make a $25,000 campaign contribution. Jackson explained his timing in coming forward—he had heard testimony from former state appointee Ali Ata at Rezko's trial about Blagojevich handing out an appointment in exchange for a $25,000 campaign contribution.

When Jackson was asked to come in and formally provide his information on possible wrongdoing by the governor, he told prosecutors it would have to wait until after Blagojevich made his decision on whom to appoint to the U.S. Senate. Jackson wanted Blagojevich to choose him.

Now, here was Glockner on the phone, and he had questions. A thoroughly anxious Jackson peppered Glockner with questions: Was he accused of wrongdoing? Was he under arrest? Was the investigation targeting him?

Jackson wasn't charged or even a target at the time.

But there were tapes. And for some reason, Blagojevich believed the congressman was ready to give him money in exchange for the Senate seat. The key section of the charging papers involving Jackson said this: "In a recorded conversation on October 31, 2008, Rod Blagojevich described an earlier approach by an associate of Senate Candidate 5 as follows: 'We were approached pay-to-play. That, you know, he'd raise me 500 grand. An emissary came. Then the other guy would raise a million, if I made him [Senate Candidate 5] a senator.'"

The section said further that on December 4, 2008, Blagojevich told his brother in a recorded call to meet with Nayak, referred to as "Individual D," to ask about giving "tangible political support" for Jackson's appointment. The next day, after the *Chicago Tribune* published a story reporting that the government was recording Blagojevich, the ex-governor told his own brother to "undo that [Nayak] thing."

Now, the feds wanted to know: Why was Blagojevich ever under the impression that he'd get money if he appointed the congressman to the Senate seat?

Jackson said he lobbied hard and heavily for the seat, but he never crossed the line and never told anyone else to do so. He said he never offered to raise money for Blagojevich.

On that same day, Jackson reached out to someone with whom he sometimes butted heads: his father. The younger Jackson had repeatedly attempted to distinguish himself from his father, including distancing himself when he didn't like something the Reverend was doing. This dynamic came into play when the Reverend was inadvertently heard saying, while waiting to tape a segment on Fox News, that he wanted to cut then-candidate Barack Obama's "nuts off" for "talking down to black people."

"I'm deeply outraged and disappointed in Reverend Jackson's reckless statements about Senator Barack Obama," the younger Jackson said at the time. "His divisive and demeaning comments about the presumptive Democratic nominee—and I believe the next president of the United States—contradict his inspiring and courageous career...I thoroughly reject and repudiate his ugly rhetoric. He should keep hope alive and any personal attacks and insults to himself."

The day of Blagojevich's arrest, though, was a different story. The Reverend, too, had a long-term relationship with Nayak. The two had traveled to India together. Nayak first met the Jacksons through Jesse Jr.'s brother Jonathan. He contributed to Jackson's congressional campaign and formed a company with Jonathan Jackson, 6760 Stony Island LLC. Nayak also became one of several major contributors and fundraisers for Blagojevich from Chicago's Indian community.

It was Jonathan's cell phone number that called Nayak in the late afternoon the day the governor was arrested. The voice on the line, though, was an aide to the Reverend. The elder Jackson didn't want to talk on Nayak's line, so Nayak used his wife's phone to return the call. (Ultimately, Nayak gave the feds all of his cell phone records, as well as his wife's.) Eventually, Nayak was on the phone with both the Reverend and Jesse Jr., who had media lighting up his phone lines and staking out his front lawn.

Jackson asked Nayak if the FBI had approached him about the criminal complaint. Was Nayak Individual D? Nayak told the Jacksons the FBI had been to his house but he had told them that the congressman had made no illicit requests of him and that he had not made an offer to the governor.

Even after being reassured by the conversation with Nayak, Jackson still had to deal with the media inferno. He made a public statement addressing the criminal complaint and distancing himself from the accusations.

"I did not initiate or authorize anyone at any time to promise anything to Governor Blagojevich on my behalf," Jackson said right after the arrest. "I never sent a message or an emissary to the governor to make an offer, to plead my case, or to propose a deal about a U.S. Senate seat, period. I thought, mistakenly, that the process was fair, aboveboard, and on the merits. I thought, mistakenly, that the governor was evaluating me and other Senate hopefuls based upon our credentials and qualifications."

Jackson admitted the day after the governor's arrest that he was the person identified as Senate Candidate 5 in the criminal complaint against Blagojevich. But the congressman said he did nothing wrong and still wanted to replace Obama. Jackson joined the chorus asking for Blagojevich's resignation and calling for him to give up his power to pick Obama's replacement. Jackson told reporters of the conversation with the U.S. Attorney's office.

"They shared with me that I am not a target of this investigation, and that I am not accused of any misconduct," he said. In one part of the government's charging papers, authorities said that Blagojevich authorized his brother to meet with Jackson's emissary—presumably Nayak—and demand that the money start flowing.

"Some of this stuff's gotta start happening now…right now…and we gotta see it," Blagojevich told his brother. "You understand?"

For days, the "emissary" was not identified. The press besieged the Reverend about whether he was the emissary. It reached the point where he issued a statement later during the week of the governor's arrest.

"Our office has received calls today inquiring about or suggesting that I or a member of my family served as an emissary in Governor Blagojevich's 'pay-to-play' scheme, revealed through wiretaps, to fill the state's open Senate seat," he said. "It is not true."

That same week, Jackson Jr. seemed to indicate to the *Sun-Times* that he had no plans to sever ties with Nayak.

"All my life I have watched people abandon people at their most difficult and desperate hours," he said. "He's a very affluent man. He doesn't need to do anything illegal. I pray for him and I am confident I didn't ask him to do anything that is suggested in the complaint that would violate the law."

Days later, Nayak and his lawyer contacted federal authorities. Nayak had something he wanted to tell them.

He had lied to agents about Jackson.

Politicos often used Nayak, who owned several surgical centers in Illinois and Indiana, for his deep pockets. He was left holding the bill for at least one campaign fundraiser that Blagojevich didn't pay for, and he paid many a bill for the Jacksons. He liked feeling close to power.

Now, though, Nayak and his attorney, a former federal prosecutor named Thomas K. McQueen, were meeting with agents in a downtown office. In that meeting, Nayak told authorities a dramatically different story than what they had heard from Jackson. He said he approached the governor's brother, at Jackson's direction, on October 31, 2008, with a multimillion-dollar offer for the Senate seat. The story went back to an October 8, 2008, visit to Washington, D.C., where Nayak had gone for a special signing of the U.S.–India Nuclear Cooperation Act at the White House. Nayak was a backer of this effort, which was aimed at bringing electricity to rural India. Before heading to the White House, though, he went to Jackson's Washington, D.C., home.

Jackson called a limo to pick up the two for lunch, according to Nayak. Jackson wanted to go to the Cheesecake Factory. It was at this lunch, Nayak said, that Jackson started talking about the Senate seat. Nayak described Jackson as aggressive and power hungry, saying that he discussed how easily he could raise campaign money if he were a U.S. senator.

He then made a proposal, according to Nayak: Jackson told Nayak to tell Blagojevich that if he named Jackson to the Senate seat, the Indian community in Chicago would raise $1 million for him. And, once Jackson was named to the Senate, he would raise another $5 million for Blagojevich.

We can't raise that, Nayak said he told Jackson. It didn't matter, Jackson told Nayak; tell Blagojevich that anyway. But there was more to Jackson's proposal. Jackson told Nayak to tell Blagojevich that the two of them could run on the same ticket in the next election, in 2010, and that Jackson would make sure that the Reverend James Meeks—who could potentially divide the black vote—didn't challenge Blagojevich in the gubernatorial race.

Jackson also spoke of Obama, according to Nayak. He told Nayak that he and Obama were close and that Obama would be willing to help Jackson. If it came to it, Jackson told Nayak, he would leverage his friendship with Obama to get a pardon for Blagojevich, according to Nayak.

Jackson's limo driver took Nayak directly to the White House, where the congressman and Nayak posed together for a picture in front of the gates. Nayak gave the feds a copy of the picture, and it would later be entered into evidence.

There was another portion of Nayak's talk with the feds that may have concerned Jackson. That involved Giovanna Huidobro, a stunning blonde Peruvian who sometimes modeled. Photos depicting her in a bikini were easily found on the Internet. When Nayak visited Washington, Huidobro rode in the limousine with Jackson. Then the three of them dined together on October 8, 2008—the same day that Nayak had told authorities he had a key conversation with Jackson about the Senate appointment. The three ended up at Ozio, a restaurant and club where Huidobro worked and where Jackson had held fundraisers. Nayak told authorities that Jackson had asked him to pay for plane tickets so Huidobro could fly to Chicago. Nayak said he twice paid for her flights at Jackson's request. He gave authorities copies of his credit card statements.

The following March, it was Jackson's turn to talk to the feds. He was consistent with Nayak on some points. Yes, Nayak traveled to Washington, D.C., on October 8, 2008. Yes, he and Nayak had lunch at the Cheesecake Factory. Yes, Jackson, along with Huidobro, a "social acquaintance," also later picked up Nayak from the White House in a limo. They ended up at Ozio with some of Nayak's cousins who lived nearby. Jackson, though, remained steadfast in his denials about the Senate seat. He denied ever telling Nayak to approach Blagojevich or his brother with a money offer. Jackson once said he didn't even know Blagojevich had a brother.

But as the *Sun-Times* investigated what happened in Jackson's interview, it became clear that another headache was building. Sources were saying they had caught wind of a congressional ethics inquiry into Jackson. Ultimately, on the day of Blagojevich's indictment in 2009, the Office of Congressional Ethics, formed just the previous year, voted to conduct a "preliminary review" of actions surrounding Jackson's bid to be appointed to the Senate seat.

Nayak's description of the $6-million offer was far different than what investigators were hearing play out on tapes. They heard Blagojevich refer to a $1.5-million offer from Jackson's people. As it turned out, none of Nayak's allegations became public before Blagojevich's 2010 trial. As the trial approached, it was unclear whether Nayak would be called to the witness stand by either the defense or the prosecution.

Jackson and his father still seemed concerned about the case, though. The two were seen heading in and out of the Monadnock Building, a historic skyscraper around the corner from the Dirksen Federal Courthouse. The Monadnock Building was filled with the offices of defense lawyers—including the office where the two would stop, that of Ed Genson.

There was another piece to the Jackson puzzle: Robert Blago-jevich. He was at the helm of his brother's campaign fund when he was approached by two separate people—Nayak and another fundraiser named Rajinder Bedi—who both talked of an offer of campaign money in exchange for Jackson's appointment.

These approaches happened three months after Rob took over his brother's campaign fund. He would later testify from the witness stand and back up some of the details Nayak conveyed to federal authorities, including the fact that the amount of money discussed was $6 million, not $1.5 million. Rob said he was approached by Nayak at an October 31, 2008, fundraising meeting. Nayak promised that if the governor appointed Jackson, $1 million would be raised for Blagojevich by the end of 2008 and then another $5 million would go to Blagojevich after Jackson became senator.

Rob Blagojevich testified that three days before the October 31 meeting with Nayak, he met with Bedi, who was managing director of the state's Office of Trade and Investment. Rob said Bedi told him that if his brother appointed Jackson to the Senate seat, he would get $1 million in campaign money. Bedi, who testified at Blagojevich's trial for the prosecution, said he had the conversation with Rob hours after he'd had a breakfast meeting with Jackson. At the Jackson meeting, where Nayak was also present, Nayak told Jackson he'd raise $1 million for Blagojevich if Jackson were appointed senator.

Rob said he relayed the information from Bedi to his brother. Rob referred to the fundraisers from the Indian community as clumsy "Keystone Cops" whom he easily dismissed.

"We thought it was just a joke," Rob testified of Bedi's overture. "It was outrageous." He said he didn't recall telling his brother of Nayak's subsequent $6-million offer.

"We dealt with the issue on the 28th," Rob told his lawyer Michael Ettinger at trial. "It was dead."

The feds followed up on their interviews with Nayak, whose allegations against Jackson were tremendous. But Nayak was the only witness to this pay-to-play conversation. They couldn't go put a congressman on trial for that alone.

Nayak had his own issues. Bedi, his longtime friend, was also spilling his guts to the feds. And Bedi gave them a piece of information that Nayak hadn't: Nayak ran a check-cashing scheme. From 2003 to 2008 he had paid Bedi close to $2 million for doing nothing, and in return, Bedi gave Nayak about $1.4 million back in cash. Bedi said he thought Nayak was trying to evade paying taxes on the money.

"I think his tax bracket was about 30 percent," Bedi later said at Blagojevich's trial. There was also an investigation into Nayak's surgical centers, which were said to have paid out improper finder's fees.

In 2009 the feds interviewed Huidobro. They were trying to determine whether she had heard anything from Jackson on the day that Nayak said he had that critical conversation with the congressman. Had she heard of an offer to the Blagojevich campaign for cash in exchange for the then-governor appointing Jackson to the seat once held by President Obama? She told authorities she knew nothing of Jackson's political dealings regarding the Senate seat. She did say she flew to Chicago on several occasions at Jackson's request, and that Jackson sometimes reimbursed her for her travels. Jackson did not report the flights for Huidobro as gifts on his House financial-disclosure statement. The feds saw that as an ethical violation at best.

Following the charges against Blagojevich, Jackson's public appearances were few.

When Blagojevich's 2010 trial finally arrived, there was public testimony that Jackson was at the table when Nayak and Bedi talked about the Senate seat and fundraising for Blagojevich.

Bedi said he met Jackson on numerous occasions, usually when he was with Nayak.

"I seen him on events if Raghu Nayak was doing [*sic*] at his home, or if those events were elsewhere where Raghu Nayak may have hosted an event for him, or if it was an event organized by Jesse Jackson Jr., where he was invited and then I may have gone with Raghu Nayak to these events," Bedi said, explaining, "[t]hose were fundraisers."

Prosecutor Christopher Niewoehner asked Bedi to describe Nayak and Jackson's relationship.

"Very close relationship," Bedi said. Bedi said he attended the Democratic National Convention with Nayak and, together, they hung out in Jackson's suite. How was it that he was invited to Jackson's suite?

"Because of the relationship that Raghu Nayak has with the family," said Bedi.

Turning to the 2008 breakfast meeting, Bedi explained that Blagojevich had asked him to speak with Jackson about a project for an airport in Peotone, Illinois. Bedi asked Nayak to help arrange the meeting. On October 27, Bedi said Nayak told him he was going to meet the congressman the next day "in your neighborhood," at a restaurant called 312 at Randolph and LaSalle. The next day, Bedi did meet with Jackson, and he said that a member of Jackson's staff—his "district director" and driver—was sitting at another table. Jackson's staff member was "in and out. He was working on something. They would talk briefly, he would go, he would come back. He would sit."

Eventually, Nayak showed up as promised, Bedi said. Jackson spoke passionately and at length about the Peotone airport.

"After Nayak joined the conversation, did Congressman Jackson talk about a different topic?" Niewoehner asked.

"Yes, for some time the conversation about this South Side development continued and then we ended that and at that time we three were sitting and there was conversation about Jesse Jackson Jr.'s interest in getting appointed to the Senate seat, which would eventually be vacated by Barack Obama if he became president of the United States."

The key question came: "What did Congressman Jackson say about his interest in what might become the vacant Senate seat?"

The answer, though, was blocked. Rob Blagojevich's attorney, Michael Ettinger, objected based on hearsay.

The courtroom was cleared and, without the jury present, the judge decided what could be allowed in the testimony. Niewoehner said, "In a nutshell, the thing that is significant is they talk about the Senate seat for a bit, [and] Nayak says to Jackson in Bedi's presence, 'I will raise a million dollars for Rod Blagojevich if he appoints you to the Senate seat.'" That led Bedi to talk to Rob Blagojevich about the offer later that same day, Niewoehner explained.

"That is the heart of our case, essentially," Niewoehner told Judge James Zagel. "That they understand that that is the offer on the table and then there is a number of conversations that we are going to elicit between Rob and Rod where they discuss—they and other people talk about a particular offer."

Eventually, Bedi was allowed only to say that fundraising was discussed at the meeting with Jackson and that, the same day, he told Rob Blagojevich about a $1-million offer to appoint Jackson to the Senate seat.

That was as far as it went. Jackson wasn't called as a witness. Neither was Nayak. Jackson got some bad publicity on that day. Ultimately, though, the allegations involving Jackson and Blagojevich, such as they were, didn't gain much traction. Things seemed to be looking up for the congressman.

In September 2010, Jackson, speaking on WLS-AM's Don Wade and Roma show, responded for the first time publicly to an allegation that he was present at an October 28, 2008, meeting with Bedi and Nayak where fundraising for Blagojevich and the Senate seat came up.

On the radio show, Jackson said that he didn't participate in the talk, and he did not hear it.

"I'm not alone at the meeting. It baffled me, you know: 'Jackson sits alone with the Indians,'" he said, referring to media coverage after testimony at Blagojevich's trial.

"How about this? Congressman meets with Director of Economic Development and Trade for the State of Illinois [Bedi].... [He] met with him for 30 minutes in the presence of other people and discussed the third airport. Then another gentleman showed up and started having another conversation practically in Hindu [*sic*], because I don't speak Hindu...and I didn't participate in any of that part of the conversation, nor do I even remember hearing it. And I have witnesses present.

(*Hindi* is the predominant language in India. The word "Hindu" refers to an adherent of the religion Hinduism.)

Bedi, a government witness, did not testify that he was speaking in Hindi.

When the feds interviewed Bedi, he told them Jackson was engaged in the conversation. Jackson expounded on raising money for a Senate campaign, according to Bedi, and discussed how powerful he would be if he were the only African American in the Senate.

Jackson was also asked in the radio interview about a closed-door meeting with Rahm Emanuel. There was a rumor that the two cut a deal to avoid discussing Blagojevich should they go head to head in a campaign battle to become mayor of Chicago. Still, Jackson didn't waste time throwing the first stone in the radio interview. He noted that Emanuel was caught on secretly recorded FBI tapes, and pointed out that he himself was not. Jackson said he still worried about the Blagojevich retrial taking place the following year, but only because it would distract from the issues.

"The prosecution has concluded, I assume, that what I have to say doesn't contribute to their case," Jackson said. "I assume they have no evidence, or else they would have brought a charge. If I'm a conspirator, bring it on."

That same day, two *Sun-Times* reporters called Jackson's office. They laid out what they had been investigating since the beginning of the year involving the congressman. It wasn't pretty. The following week, the *Sun-Times* disclosed that Nayak, whose closeness to the Jacksons was publicly known by now, told authorities that Jackson had directed him to make a pay-to-play offer to the Blagojevich camp. Before this, it was unclear whether anyone had ever made that accusation about Jackson; Jackson himself had portrayed the recordings as perhaps the result of someone acting out of school on his behalf but without his authority.

Nayak's lawyer confirmed that his client had talked to the FBI about the October 8 meeting and that Nayak provided documents to authorities involving his dealings with Jackson. The *Sun-Times* ran the photo of Nayak and the congressman posing together in front of the White House on October 8.

What really made the story go viral, though, was the revelation that Nayak had paid to fly a "social acquaintance" of Jackson's to and from Washington in October and December 2008 at Jackson's request. The blogosphere lit up. A few used the headline "Jesse's Girl" with sultry photos of Huidobro alongside the posts. Some in the African-American community were particularly upset, perhaps because Huidobro is white.

Both the congressman and his wife responded to the news that same day. Jackson was resolved to stay in office, but apologized to his constituency. He referred to his relationship with Huidobro as a "private and personal matter," but never used the words "mistress" or "affair." He said he was "deeply sorry."

"The allegations about fundraising and the Senate seat are not new. I've already talked with the authorities about these claims, told them they were false, and no charges have been brought against me," Jackson said in a written statement that day. "The very idea of raising millions of dollars for a campaign other than my own is preposterous. My interest in the Senate seat was based on years of public service, which I am proud of, not some improper scheme with anyone.

"The reference to a social acquaintance is a private and personal matter between me and my wife that was handled some time ago. I ask that you respect our privacy. I know I have disappointed some supporters and for that I am deeply sorry. But I remain committed to serving my constituents and fighting on their behalf."

While Jackson said he dealt with the matter "some time ago," it was unclear when he had discussed Huidobro with his wife. For her part, Sandi Jackson put out a statement early in the day. It appeared on other news sites and indicated that the two had dealt with the matter "months ago." The *Sun-Times* asked for a copy of the statement later in the day.

When the *Sun-Times* received it, something had changed. Now the statement said that the couple had been dealing with the issue for two years.

Sandi eventually spoke publicly on the matter in more detail. In an interview with *Sun-Times* columnist Michael Sneed, she said, "I'd known about it nearly two years ago because Jesse told me late one night in our home in Washington," she said. "When Jesse told me about the indiscretion, I didn't want details. I know what adultery looks like. I didn't need to visualize it. I needed to concentrate on my kids.

"He said it was over. I was mortified and in agony, but he knew if I found out any other way it would be over," Sandi said then. "That the only way to save our marriage was to come clean."

There was one more confounding aspect to the investigation involving Jackson and Nayak. Nayak told authorities that after Jackson directed him to make a money offer for the Senate seat, he received another phone call from the congressman in November. Nayak said Jackson warned him that there was a federal investigation into the U.S. Senate seat selection and that he shouldn't make any pay-to-play offers to Blagojevich. At that point, the investigation was top secret, given the covert wiretap operation.

Nayak's statement suggested that Jackson, a potential subject of the probe, had somehow caught wind of it. Nayak said he told Jackson he had already made the approach, at which point Jackson told him not to worry.

Backing up Nayak's contention was Bedi, whom the prosecution put on the witness stand. In debriefing sessions with the government, Bedi, who had told the government about wrongdoing by Nayak, said Nayak called him in November after being warned by Jackson about the federal investigation.

For his part, Jackson told authorities he didn't know about the probe ahead of time, although, he also said, he figured there was some kind of federal oversight going on. He told the feds he knew they were listening.

Chapter Five

Brothers Grim

The reality sank in for Rob Blagojevich. He was part of this mess.

He had spent years as a military officer and then building up his career in banking and real estate, staying out of his brother's political life as Rod Blagojevich was ascending from state lawmaker to congressman to governor. In 2006, he volunteered during his brother's second-term gubernatorial campaign run, canvassing neighborhoods and fundraising in ethnic communities. Then, at his brother's request, Rob agreed in August 2008 to head his brother's campaign fund.

By the following spring, he was under federal indictment on two wire-fraud charges. The two brothers were expected to face trial in a Chicago courtroom together.

It was a few months earlier in that same year that Rob had gone back to the University of Tampa, his alma mater, to give the commencement speech. The successful Nashville businessman and longtime military officer saw it as a special moment.

He was honored to have been asked back to the school where he had fallen in love with his future wife, Julie, over long talks in the library. Afterward, Rob sat with Julie along a breezy boulevard, soaking in the good feelings and the warm air.

"We thought our lives had peaked," he recalled. "We sat there in the breeze, saying how good life was."

When Rob and Julie came to Chicago, they stayed in a condo used by their son, Alex. Julie was a private person. When the former beauty queen from Florida learned their home had been taped, she was overcome by a "horrifying, sick, sick feeling" and burst into tears. She imagined strangers listening in on her private conversations for months.

"What might I have said that was out of school?" she thought. "What might I have said thinking it was a private conversation between Rob and me about a family member, about a friend, about my work, about anything?"

Now Rob was looking for a criminal defense lawyer. He wanted someone aggressive, experienced—someone who wouldn't cave to the U.S. Attorney's office. He picked prominent federal defense expert Michael Ettinger.

As personalities go, Ettinger and Rob were an unlikely pairing. Rob looked more like someone who lifts weights regularly, drinks his milk, and apologizes after swearing. Ettinger, a gravelly voiced, plainspoken smoker, unapologetically drops f-bombs when referring to federal prosecutors. He had been around the federal courts building for decades and knew how things worked. And he didn't hesitate to attack the government's case. Ettinger thought the government's evidence against Rob was thin. Ettinger wasn't afraid to wage a war, and Rob liked that.

Prosecutors at one point approached Rob's legal team, saying they would like to find a "global resolution" to the legal ordeal. How would that happen? The governor would have to fold. Or— Ettinger assumed, reading between the lines—they wanted Rob to testify against his brother. When asked at the time if it were a possibility, Ettinger didn't hesitate: "Not a prayer."

People in Illinois didn't know much about Rob Blagojevich. It was assumed he was another version of Rod. And there was immediate chatter about the large chunk of change he pulled in per month as the head of the campaign fund—$12,500.

Rob was a lifelong Republican who, after all his years in Nashville, talked with a slight Southern drawl. Unlike his brother, he stayed out of the limelight. Five months after his indictment, seething about what they viewed as a monumental intrusion and overreach by federal authorities, Julie and Rob agreed to sit down with the *Sun-Times* at Ettinger's office in Palos Heights, Illinois, for their first public interview. Rob agreed to be photographed, but politely remarked that he didn't think it was a good idea to be quoted since he was a defendant in the case. If the reporter had general questions for his wife, though, that would be fine.

Among the first questions asked: Why on earth did Rob agree to join his brother after it was crystal clear that the feds were investigating his administration? The governor had long been dogged by investigations, which led to the indictments of his two top former fundraisers, one of whom was Rezko.

"We knew about allegations, and we knew about investigations," Julie Blagojevich began. "Rod assured us that he was not doing anything wrong. We understood that the allegations were really behind him, the investigation was really behind him." Taking the job in Chicago would also give them the chance to spend more time with their 26-year-old son, Alex. She insisted that taking the job had nothing to do with money. Her husband was successful on his own in Nashville. And he'd be trying to maintain his real estate business while working for Rod in Chicago.

Julie said she gave Rob her OK to help Rod because of her late mother-in-law, Millie. She had always told Julie that the brothers should stick together. "When we're gone, you two only have each other," Julie said her mother-in-law would tell her boys. Millie Blagojevich had often cried to her sons about her own brothers and how they'd grown estranged.

"She never wanted that to happen to her two sons," Julie said. "It was important to me for Rob and Rod to maintain a good relationship." Julie said she'd listened to all the tapes and was confounded by the charges. She insisted there was nothing on the tapes that would warrant criminal charges against her husband.

"I am frustrated with the government because I believe he is being held hostage by them," Julie said. "I believe that they indicted Rob to get his brother to plead. My husband is an innocent man, wrongly accused. He's done nothing wrong. He's been portrayed to be the bagman for his brother....He is so not that person. He's the most honorable, forthright, direct,...moral person you will ever, ever meet."

There seemed to be an additional undercurrent to Julie's responses: that Rod didn't appreciate his older brother, recognize Rob's loyalty, or validate his private-sector success.

"It was also important to me to hope that Rod might see what a wonderful brother he has," Julie said.

There was, however, the matter of the tapes. The charges said that the ex-governor instructed his brother to tell Nayak that he needed to see something tangible, up front, if he wanted the governor to appoint Jackson to the Senate.

"You gotta be careful how you express that, and assume everybody's listening, the whole world is listening," Blagojevich was overheard telling Rob on a wiretapped conversation. "You hear me?"

Rob agreed and then called Nayak to set up a meeting. Nayak said the two could meet that day. Let's do it tomorrow, Rob told him.

A law enforcement official who didn't want to be named said of the decision to charge Rob, "We believed he had known about some of the shakedowns, he was not completely ignorant. He knew right from wrong. He was no dummy."

As the questions came during the interview, Rob couldn't help but chime in.

"Let me tell you what really happened—and you can quote me," he'd say. Eventually, the dam broke. Rob made it clear that his relationship with his brother was strained. He said he felt betrayed by the government for invading his home. They taped all kinds of personal conversations, he contended—husband and wife, father and son, talk that had nothing to do with the case at hand. They even taped a private conversation with his son where the agents could hear his son going to the bathroom.

Rob Blagojevich projected an air of authority. He had spent 21 years in the U.S. Army and took it as a personal affront that the country he served had turned on him. He said investigators were combing through his financials, sending subpoenas to his accountant, asking for documents. He was confident they'd find nothing.

"We're not perfect people, but I'm not a criminal," he said. "This is just not fair. It's absolutely not fair."

Though his brother frustrated him, Rob said he'd never turn on him. "I do not plan to plead guilty. I plan to go to trial. We're codefendants, and we are not guilty on those charges," he said. "I would not testify against my brother." Rob pointed to an exchange the previous November between himself and Roland Burris, who eventually got the Senate appointment. The secretly recorded conversation was made public as part of a U.S. Senate ethics inquiry into Burris. Burris can be heard telling Rob that he's feeling conflicted, that he wants to give to the Blagojevich campaign fund but is worried how it would look as he seeks the Senate seat appointment.

On tape, Rob presses Burris to donate to his brother. But, regarding the Senate seat, he clarifies he wants to "manage expectations," telling Burris that many others also are seeking it.

"How I conducted myself with Burris is how I conducted myself with everyone when no one was looking," he said.

The Blagojevich brothers grew up near Armitage and Cicero in Chicago. Their immigrant father was born outside Belgrade and served in the Serbian army. Their Chicago-born mother was the daughter of Serbian immigrants. As kids, the Blagojevich brothers played in a Serbian orchestra, where Rod sometimes also sang.

"Rod took after my dad, had a great voice," Rob told the *Sun-Times* in 2006. "He had the balls to get up there and do it."

The two pulled many pranks. Once, they took some broken-up bits of plasterboard and scrawled all over the brick wall of a Pentecostal Church next door to their home.

When their father got home, they were in trouble. They "dutifully cleaned it up, feeling stupid," Rob recalled. "We were never arrested. We were never in jeopardy of being at odds with the police, never even came close to that. But we did a lot of stuff, prankster stuff, the kind of stuff you shake your head at and say, 'How did we get away with that?'"

The brothers were tight growing up in Chicago. Rob said he played the part of big brother easily. He came to his brother's aid when Rod mouthed off to bigger kids in the neighborhood—a common occurrence.

But when he left for college in Tampa, he said he and his brother grew apart. "We didn't really know each other as adults," Rob said. "I left Chicago to go to college. I never came back except as a visitor. We were very, very close growing up. But then he went his way, and I went mine."

Rob won a military scholarship and, after graduating cum laude, went on active military duty. By 25, he was living in Germany and was in charge of three Pershing nuclear missiles. After his military career, he settled in Tennessee and his career in financial services took off. At one point, he was in charge of $3.5 billion in trust assets with First American, then Tennessee's biggest bank.

Meanwhile, his little brother bounced around to different colleges before going to law school and eventually entering Chicago politics. Rod wasn't the one winning the scholarships in this family, Rob said, laughing.

"It's our job to focus on what Rob did, and that's how we're going to defend it," said his lawyer, Michael Ettinger.

Rob initially faced five counts, including allegations he discussed extracting a $1.5-million campaign donation from an emissary to Jesse Jackson Jr. in exchange for the Senate appointment. The former governor faced more extensive charges, 25 counts in all, from mail fraud to making false statements.

While Rob headed his brother's campaign fund, it was Rod who was able to use it to bankroll his legal costs. Rob had to dip into his own pockets to pay for his defense. Although there was coolness and frustration between them after they were charged, Rob still lent his kid brother a car following his impeachment.

"It'll be eternal brotherly love," Rob Blagojevich said. "That's never going to go away. Rod's a big boy, I'm a big boy. He can take care of himself. I got a lot of confidence that he'll be able to without me, you know, or with me. I mean, since we're codefendants— together. Otherwise, he's a big boy, he can take care of himself. I don't mean that in any negative way. He's a survivor."

The media spectacle was in place around the Dirksen Federal Courthouse downtown on the morning of April 14, 2009. It was the first time the ex-governor would enter the building for a scheduled hearing since his spectacular December 9 arrest, when he showed up in a jogging suit and left escorted by his security. On this day, he was to enter the building as a private citizen.

Courtroom security, in preparing for Blagojevich and ordering that no special arrangements be made on his behalf, referred to him in a prepared release as "Mr. Blagojevich." Meanwhile, past the media, down the sidewalk, across the street inside the historic Monadnock Building, sat Rob Blagojevich, his defense team seated around him. Pale-faced and occasionally letting out deep sighs, Rob insisted he wasn't nervous. He sipped coffee as he spoke deliberately.

"I'm prepared," he said plainly. He walked through the media fray, went upstairs to the 25th floor and, together with his brother, pleaded not guilty to a federal criminal indictment.

Chapter Six

A Governor in Court

Instead of wearing a jogging suit, Rod Blagojevich wore a pin-striped suit and a blue tie. In the courtroom, he took on a serious demeanor, keeping his hands folded in front of him and answering, "I have a degree from law school," when asked about his education.

Rod and Rob Blagojevich were released on $4,500 recognizance bonds, after they were charged in a 19-count indictment. Rod Blagojevich's lawyer, Sheldon Sorosky, asked for a short court date to request a special travel permission for his client.

Moments after entering his formal plea of not guilty, the ex-governor was smiling inside the Dirksen elevator. He was on his way down to the courthouse lobby, where he knew a massive media horde awaited him. He reached out and shook this reporter's hand.

"How are you?" he asked.

When asked how he was, Blagojevich thought for a second. Then he compared himself to Winston Churchill after battle. Churchill's books lined the shelves of the ex-governor's reading room. He quoted the British statesman: "Now this is not the end.

It is not even the beginning of the end. But it is, perhaps, the end of the beginning."

Out of the elevator, into the courthouse lobby, a media scrum was waiting. He floated toward the cameras, almost instinctively, but his lawyer tugged at him to just keep walking. Blagojevich said he couldn't talk, nodding to his lawyers as if it weren't his idea.

"The truth will prevail," he called out. "I look forward to clearing my name and being vindicated." Once outside the building, he said he would take no questions. Then the shouts from reporters beckoned him.

He answered one. Then another. He was quick with a quip and got a laugh from the crowd. As he warmed up to the reporters, more people moved in around him, barely allowing him to walk. Soon, the entire courthouse sidewalk was covered with media people, Blagojevich at the center as bodies pressed forward, cameras, tape recorders, and microphones all lurching toward the ex-governor. Photographers and cameramen stood atop concrete barriers to get an overhead view.

"Oh my God," one photographer exclaimed as he looked over the swarm of bodies. A cameraman stumbled. "Fuck!" he said as he struggled to regain his balance. He looked at the ex-governor and apologized for swearing.

Blagojevich smiled. It was nothing he hadn't heard before, he said. "Listen to some of those tapes," he said.

Reporters swore as they stepped on each other's feet. Others huddled around, shoving their mics or tape recorders toward the governor without even getting anywhere near him. "He's not going to leave until the last question is asked," one TV reporter said of the raucous scene. Onlookers took out their cell phones to snap photos and videotape the mess. Others inside the courthouse stood by the glass windows, sipping coffee and taking in the spectacle.

Through it all, Rod Blagojevich kept his smile. He seemed to bask in the attention. Yes, he had been criminally charged. But when he came to court he had something else on his mind: the special travel permission Sorosky sought. Blagojevich wanted to ask the judge if he could head to the jungles of Costa Rica. The ousted governor had been invited to take part in a reality TV venture, a *Survivor*-style show *I'm a Celebrity...Get Me Out of Here!* that would be filmed that June. The prime-time NBC program promised to pay contestants tens of thousands of dollars for their involvement. There was one little detail, though: the former governor needed permission from U.S. District Judge James Zagel to travel outside the country. His bond said he couldn't leave without a judge's OK.

It was a bizarre request to make in the midst of one of the most expansive corruption cases in the history of Illinois. Blagojevich had already done his huge TV talk show blitz earlier in the year, which had seemed odd enough at the time. People now started whispering about how Costa Rica was a non-extradition country. Blagojevich, unemployed—and unemployable—since the Illinois legislature booted him from office months earlier, said he was simply looking for a way to make money. Patti had also lost her fundraising job with the Chicago Christian Industrial League.

Zagel flatly rejected Blagojevich's request, telling him he'd be better off tending to his court case. Then, he said something that was on nearly everyone's mind. "I don't think this defendant in all honesty...fully understands the position he finds himself in," Zagel said.

Blagojevich insisted he did appreciate the gravity of his case, but needed to raise money "for my kids." Later that week, Blagojevich was seen strapped to a harness, suspended in mid-air with the backdrop of a giant green screen behind him. He was in Los Angeles filming a commercial for *I'm a Celebrity...Get Me Out of*

Here! A video posted of the taping had the *Superman* theme song playing in the background as Blagojevich bounced in the air, his massive head of hair blowing wildly.

U.S. deputy marshals were increasingly aware that Blagojevich's visits to the federal building were creating a security hazard. So on this morning, the plan had been for Blagojevich to meet up with two deputy marshals at the Dunkin' Donuts across Jackson Street from the federal courthouse so they could make a clandestine approach to the building.

It didn't work so well. A few reporters noticed the deputy marshals crossing the street and pounced. That drew the media en masse, all rushing to get across the street, barely paying attention to traffic. A city bus hit its brakes as media scattered.

Blagojevich crossed Jackson Street with a crush of reporters surrounding him, most of whom were walking backward. A microphone dropped. The ex-governor crouched down to pick it up and asked, "Whose is this?"

"Thanks, governor," the reporter said.

While en route, a spectator who had waited nearby handed Blagojevich a blue Tiffany bag with a box in it. It contained a Tiffany candle and candleholder as well as a note that said, "Good luck. We know you're innocent. You did good things for the people."

"I hope that's not ticking," a security officer told Blagojevich. Once inside the building, Blagojevich assured security that the box had gone through a security scan.

As they went inside an elevator and up to the 25th floor, Blagojevich apologized to the deputy marshals for drawing the horde. They told him it wasn't his fault.

Though Blagojevich joked about taking the Tiffany box, the marshals were concerned. The marshals oversee courthouse security, including that of all the judges. They weren't in charge of protecting Blagojevich, but they also didn't have any say about his accepting potentially dangerous items like the Tiffany box he was handed that morning. The incident made it clear that courthouse security staff would have to come up with an appropriate way to handle the governor's visits, as these would become more frequent. In the elevator, the two deputies remarked that they would have to start bringing the ex-governor into the building through another location because of all the media craziness.

"But then they come to my home," Blagojevich replied.

Once on the 25th floor, the ex-governor made his way down the hallway to the north end of the building. On the way, Blagojevich saw a group of people waiting outside a courtroom not far from his. A few were Hispanic. He stopped to shake their hands and spoke to them in Spanish. Assuming they were there for a court hearing, he looked serious and sympathetic. *Buena suerte* (good luck), he said solemnly.

The crowd, unbeknownst to Blagojevich, was awaiting a swearing-in citizenship ceremony.

Chapter Seven

Consequences

A tall figure wearing a white baseball cap, blue jeans, and a navy blue T-shirt walked into a Walmart in Country Club Hills, Illinois, on September 11, 2009. A video shows the man buying a few items: Milk. Bread. A grill. Charcoal, charcoal lighter fluid.

Rat poison.

Christopher G. Kelly checked out at the Walmart cash register about 2:40 p.m., according to a police report. He walked out the front door of the store and loaded the items into his black Cadillac SUV.

About 20 minutes later, Kelly sent a text message to his girlfriend, Clarissa Flores-Buhelos. "I love 46," he wrote her, appearing to use code for the day the two met. Earlier that day, Kelly had met with his lawyer. He had talked about getting help for his depression. That meeting ended around 1:30 p.m.

Next, Kelly was at the Forest Lumber Company in Country Club Hills, where he stored machinery for his roofing business and had a trailer. Inside the trailer, with a sleeping bag on the floor, Kelly placed photos of his three daughters around him and took out the rat poison, as well as aspirin and Tylenol pills.

He then broke a promise he had made to Clarissa days earlier.

The gray-haired, blue-eyed Kelly was 51 when he pleaded guilty to a tax case in federal court in Chicago. He knew the feds wanted more from him.

Kelly, who stood six feet tall and sometimes wore glasses beneath his furrowed brow, was the father of three daughters: Grace, Jacqueline, and Claire. The roofing contractor had once lived with his kids and wife Carmen in a $2-million Burr Ridge house. But by September 2009, trouble had been brewing in his marriage for some time, and he was living with Clarissa in her downtown condo.

The previous couple of years had been devastating for the governor's former adviser, confidant, and friend. Prosecutors, hoping Kelly would flip on Blagojevich and testify against the ex-governor at trial, had thrown the book at him. Between 2007 and 2009, he was indicted three times in three different federal cases. It was a legal onslaught unlike anything many longtime courthouse observers had ever seen. Ultimately, Kelly was set to stand trial alongside Blagojevich in June 2010 on racketeering and extortion charges.

He had once been Blagojevich's go-to guy, a trusted adviser who also served as Blagojevich's finance chairman in his first campaign for governor. Their friendship dated back to before Blagojevich was a congressman. In the 1990s, Blagojevich, then a state representative, remembers seeing two men standing outside a political fundraiser. Kelly was there with his friend Ronald Rossi, who was smoking a cigar.

"I introduced myself to them," Blagojevich once told the *Sun-Times*. "It was very typical of a guy who was looking to make friends to run for Congress."

Kelly had started work in the roofing business while in his late twenties with a company called Jones & Cleary, owned by the family of his college friend, William Cleary. Kelly learned the ins and outs of the business, but had a falling-out with Cleary and left the firm in the late '90s to begin his own.

He hooked up with powerful friends who helped him land a lucrative contract at O'Hare International Airport the first time his new company, BCI Commercial Roofing, was ever listed on a bid.

During Blagojevich's first campaign for governor, Kelly, his finance chairman, helped find the millions of dollars needed for what a November 2002 *Sun-Times* article described as a "fusillade" of TV ads. But Kelly was also the member of Blagojevich's campaign team whom the candidate trusted most for an honest opinion, according to Pete Giangreco, a political consultant who was at the time part of Blagojevich's inner circle.

"More than any informal role, he was the 'Friend of the Candidate,' a guy who [Blagojevich] can look at and say, 'That speech, was it OK, or did I fuck that up?' And he could say, 'No, you fucked it up,'" Giangreco told the *Sun-Times* in 2002.

Kelly was on the train in January 2003 as Blagojevich made a "whistle-stop" trip to Springfield en route to his inauguration. Blagojevich, then 46, told a crowd in Union Station that voters gave him a mandate that was simple and clear: "No more business as usual. Shake up a system that has accepted corruption, accepted mediocrity, accepted failure whether it be on schools, whether it be on jobs, whether it be on healthcare, or whether it be on something as fundamental and basic in any relationship between people—trust." Despite Blagojevich's promise of an ethical administration, *Sun-Times* columnist Mark Brown saw Kelly as a potential bellwether for corruption, even on Blagojevich's inauguration day.

"The new governor hit many of the proper notes to set a strong ethical tone for his administration," Brown wrote, "although it probably bears noting that his campaign finance chairman, construction contractor Christopher Kelly, received the seat nearest the podium as the inauguration chairman."

Prosecutors would say later that Kelly was among the four insiders who began scheming with Blagojevich before he was elected to the governor's office in 2002. At Blagojevich's first trial, Lon Monk testified that Kelly, Blagojevich, Monk, and Tony Rezko gave themselves code names: 1, 2, 3, and 4. They met privately in a session headed by Rezko in which Rezko charted out on a dry-erase board the different ways that they could make money off the Blagojevich administration. The money was to go into a secret fund and would be tapped only once Blagojevich was no longer in office, according to Monk's testimony. Blagojevich's lawyers attacked those assertions as outrageous, and ultimately Monk could recall few details about them. Prosecutors later said it was around this time that Blagojevich ceded significant power to both Kelly and Rezko. The two were working behind the scenes to get people to pour money into the governor's campaign fund.

Less than a year into Blagojevich's tenure as governor, Kelly's murky role in Blagojevich's administration would make headlines. An October 2003 *Sun-Times* article pointed out that Kelly, Blagojevich's top gambling adviser, was a high-rolling gambler himself. Kelly didn't hesitate to wager bets worth tens of thousands of dollars at a crack.

"He understands that industry," Blagojevich said. "He goes to Vegas. He likes all of that." The article questioned Kelly's ties to the state's casinos and their impact on his official position. At the time, Kelly was raising millions of dollars for Blagojevich in relative anonymity. The article also shed light on his company's lucrative contracts at O'Hare International Airport.

Kelly described himself as "just a roofer." Blagojevich called Kelly savvy, smart, effective, and "a friend who I trust." Their kids drew Blagojevich and Kelly closer. Their daughters grew up playing together. The same bond that grew between the two men, however, created a distance between Blagojevich and his powerful father-in-law.

Alderman Richard Mell, Patti's father, was the man whose political muscle in the city helped propel Blagojevich to Illinois's highest elected office. But in January 2005, Mell and Blagojevich publicly butted heads, and Mell would use Kelly's name while airing the family's dirty laundry. He said he had been replaced within Blagojevich's political circle by Kelly, who at the time was Blagojevich's fundraising chief. Mell didn't like the way Blagojevich was handling things. Mell didn't feel he was just family; he felt he was the main reason Blagojevich had become governor.

But his son-in-law started acting more and more entitled. Blagojevich didn't like it when Mell started putting his son-in-law's name on the 33rd Ward stationery. Blagojevich's former chief legal counsel sent a letter saying it was illegal to list the governor's name on a Chicago ward's letterhead, and to remove it.

"Instead of calling me and saying, 'Why are you doing this?,' he [Blagojevich] had Chris Kelly call me and say, 'The governor is real mad at this.' And I said, 'Mad at what? A goofy name on a letterhead? This is the most bizarre thing I ever heard,'" Mell said.

In an interview with *Sun-Times* reporter Fran Spielman, Mell compared himself to a spurned spouse replaced by a trophy wife.

"It's like the case of the individual who marries his childhood sweetheart [who]... helped him get through law school or med school or become an actor," Mell said.

"Fast-forward 20 years; now he's at the top of his profession. He's a famous doctor. He's the president of the bar association. He gets nominated for an Academy Award. He and the wife now come home from the event, and he says, 'What a great man I am.' And she says, 'Wait a second, I remember you when you were crying that we needed more money or you were crying that you thought you'd fail one of the tests.' He, with his gigantic ego, cannot stand that anymore, so he jettisons that wife and gets a new trophy wife. I am the old wife. The new wife is Chris Kelly."

It was then that Mell lodged an incredible assertion that would forever change the dynamic in the Mell-Blagojevich family—and the public's perception of the governor's administration. Mell told Spielman that the governor "raises $50,000 at a crack from his ace fundraiser, Chris Kelly, who trades appointments to commissions for checks of $50,000" to the governor's political fund. The allegation was astounding, not least because it came from the governor's own father-in-law.

Kelly immediately rebuffed Mell's attacks.

"I am saddened that Alderman Mell would be making such wildly untrue accusations. I am sure he is angry, but that anger does not justify him making defamatory statements for which he will ultimately be held accountable," Kelly said. On January 14, 2005, Kelly reiterated that the allegations against him were false and threatened legal action against Mell if he didn't retract them.

"It's sad that these allegations have brought us to where we are today," Kelly said. "That being said, the allegations are 100 percent false."

Mell did hold a news conference and retreated.

"I was probably hurt and upset, and so I said things that probably in retrospect I should not have said, Mell told reporters. Mell showed reporters at the news conference a letter he wrote to Lisa Madigan and then-Cook County State's Attorney Richard Devine where he called his earlier remarks an "exaggerated extrapolation made…in the heat of the moment.

"My comments were based upon my misreading of earlier published reports," he continued. "I have, in fact, no personal knowledge now or then of any contributions being made in exchange for any board or commission appointments.…It was never my intention to impugn your reputation. I know that you would never compromise your integrity."

Kelly seemed satisfied.

"Alderman Mell has admitted his mistake. I required that he do that or be forced to tell his story in a court of law. The truth is not negotiable and we stood our ground and the truth has emerged," said Kelly. He called the two weeks after Mell's initial statements "unnecessarily trying on me and my family."

Blagojevich, meanwhile, used the Mell spat to assert his independence from his father-in-law, whose power cast a long shadow over the governor. It was at a news conference in May 2005 that Blagojevich uttered one of his most memorable lines. The governor said that Mell had conveyed "threats" to him through third parties as he was contemplating closing a landfill that his father-in-law wanted open.

"This is the kind of thing that I think, frankly, separates the men from the boys in leadership," Blagojevich said. Then, smiling, Blagojevich added, "Do you have the testicular virility to make a decision like that, knowing what's coming your way?"

"Testicular virility" drew laughter from gubernatorial staffers. The clip was played over and over on news channels that night— and many more—as Blagojevich's public family woes continued. Blagojevich credited himself for doing the right thing for the environment by shutting down the landfill. "[Mell] then went out and made a false accusation that, under threat of a defamation lawsuit, he ultimately admitted was a lie," Blagojevich said. "There's a method of operation by people like him, and they've been doing it in politics for years, and they like to leverage and probe and threaten and bluster and bully until they get their way."

Mell didn't respond to Blagojevich's comments that day. But an aide at the time said he was "hot" over them. Blagojevich ended his news conference saying he wasn't worried about any investigation.

"We're as clean as a hound's tooth," he said. "I can't wait for them to be able to conclude and vindicate all the things that we do."

As the investigations into the Blagojevich administration deepened, the feds built a case against Kelly. They used a bookie and onetime friend of Kelly's to cooperate with them. That helped them get a better picture of where Kelly's money went, and where it came from. In December 2007, Kelly was indicted for the first time, accused of underreporting his income and using corporate funds to pay off personal gambling debts.

According to prosecutors, Kelly used his roofing business to pay gambling debts to bookies. They said he disguised one payment as a company loan. In another case, he paid off a casino debt by noting in his company's books that the payment was an expense from a roofing contract with an airline. The charges also said Kelly used his company to pay for home additions, lawn maintenance, hardwood floors, draperies, and electronic equipment. To hide what he was doing, Kelly would cut checks to a friend, who would cash them and then return the money to Kelly. He wrote one check to his friend's four-year-old child.

No charges were made against the bookie.

The charges shook the Blagojevich administration. Blagojevich distanced himself from his friend. Kelly, once a powerful—many would say intimidating—figure, was now on the outside. He was referred to by Blagojevich's staff not by name but as "the white-haired guy."

When Rezko went to trial in 2008, the clearest evidence yet emerged that Kelly and Rezko had been shaking people down for campaign contributions in exchange for state appointments and contracts. One of the charges against Rezko that *didn't* stick was an allegation that he, Kelly, Stuart Levine, and William Cellini had conspired to shake down Hollywood producer Tom Rosenberg, who was best known for producing the Oscar-winning *Million Dollar Baby*. That charge, though, would reemerge later that year, in the fall of 2008, when the feds filed the same allegation in a case against Cellini.

Once Rezko was convicted and Cellini charged, Kelly's value to federal prosecutors as a witness was even more significant, not to testify against Blagojevich, but against Cellini—an insider who for decades had brokered backroom deals while his companies won hundreds of millions of dollars in state work. Meanwhile, word was getting around that Rezko was meeting with prosecutors.

After Blagojevich's arrest in December, speculation grew that Kelly would become part of the case against Blagojevich. But something else happened. Kelly was charged again—in a different case. On February 5, 2009, he was accused of winning $8.5 million in inflated roofing contracts from United and American Airlines at O'Hare International Airport. Federal prosecutors described a kickback scheme involving the lucrative contracts for Kelly's BCI Commercial Roofing. Prosecutors said he paid hundreds of thousands of dollars in kickbacks to get the contracts.

Two months later, in April, the feds hit him again, this time with charges in a massive case against Blagojevich. Kelly was named as a codefendant.

In the months that followed, Kelly grew despondent. He pleaded guilty in January of 2009 to the tax scheme charges, admitting he'd used corporate funds to pay off personal gambling debts. That plea agreement did not include a deal with prosecutors, a point Kelly's lawyer Michael Monico emphasized after court. "There is no agreement" for Kelly's cooperation, Monico said. "And we will not seek one."

On the morning of September 8, 2009—the day before his trial was to start on the charges involving O'Hare contracts—Kelly found out the feds wanted to revoke his bond, forcing him to be kept behind bars immediately. In a legal motion that was not public, prosecutors had asked a judge to revoke Kelly's bond after he got into a confrontation with an owner at a nightspot called V Live Night Club. At the time, sources told the *Sun-Times* the argument was over money Kelly had invested in the club; he was demanding to see its books. Flores-Buhelos was then listed as a manager and partner of the club, located in the Near Northwest Side neighborhood.

The thought of having to go to jail so soon proved enough to break the intractable Kelly. After all, Kelly knew what had happened to Rezko. After Rezko had been convicted the previous year, he had been held at the downtown lockup, which is common. But because Rezko was considered "high profile," he was put into isolation—for his own protection, he was told. Isolation was a grueling existence that meant having no interaction with others. Defense lawyers have long believed that using isolation is really a way to break down inmates the feds want to make more cooperative. The feds deny this, saying they have no power over the U.S. Bureau of Prisons. For Rezko's part, he spent 276 days in solitary confinement—about nine months. He was let out of his cell for one hour a day. This was Kelly's potential future.

"The motion pushed him over the edge," a confidant who asked not to be named told the *Sun-Times* at the time. Monico and Kelly headed to federal court, where they sat in a closed session before U.S. District Judge Charles Norgle. After that, Kelly returned to the condo he shared with Flores-Buhelos. He was quiet and acting unusually, Flores-Buhelos later told police. Kelly then left, telling Flores-Buhelos he was due back in court, and that he also planned to go see his daughters. That afternoon, Kelly pleaded guilty to the charges, in an agreement so hasty he was seen initialing the papers outside the courtroom before the hearing even began. Once it did, Norgle had to stop the hearing to allow Kelly to finish reading the agreement.

Norgle went through a list of standard questions. Norgle asked Kelly if he was being pressured into pleading guilty.

"I would be remiss if I didn't say that there was a great deal of pressure in my life right now," Kelly said, without elaborating. "But I'm doing it freely, and willingly, understandingly, knowingly conscious of the ramifications of my actions, and I'm accepting responsibility here in front of you today, Judge Norgle."

In the plea, Kelly admitted to a litany of fraud charges involving his roofing company's work as a contractor at O'Hare, including working with an insider to rig bids and fraudulently win contracts. That insider was accused of inflating the budget numbers; in return, Kelly paid him at least $450,000 in kickbacks, according to the plea.

The gambling—which included wagering tens of thousands of dollars at a time—was also a factor in the two federal cases to which Kelly pleaded guilty. Kelly's $2.1-million Burr Ridge home was in foreclosure. He admitted he doctored invoices as a way to divert money to pay off personal debts, including $700,000 that Rezko gave him to buy a home, according to charges.

Kelly agreed to pay the government $450,000. All together, he was facing about eight years behind bars and, because of the recent motion by prosecutors, he was set to surrender September 18. In the courtroom, Kelly looked withdrawn, perhaps defeated. During a break, he was asked by a reporter if he wanted to talk about what he was going through.

"Just wait," he said. "Someday, the whole truth will come out." Kelly said he had seen a *Sun-Times* story the week before about Rob Blagojevich, who talked to the paper about getting charged along with his brother. Kelly later said he thought the governor's brother was a good guy.

Then his talk turned dark.

"My life is over," he said. Kelly talked about being judged in another world and ominously suggested it didn't matter what happened "in this life." Before the night was out, he would attempt suicide.

Meanwhile, Blagojevich was in New York launching a campaign to promote his new book, *The Governor*.

The night of Kelly's plea in federal court, Flores-Buhelos heard from Kelly: he was at Forest Lumber Company in Country Club Hills, where he stored machinery for his roofing business and had a trailer. He told Flores-Buhelos he had taken some pills and fallen asleep. She immediately went to find him. The gate there was locked; Flores-Buhelos, formerly a basketball star at Whitney Young High School who later played for Northwestern University, jumped it and found Kelly acting strangely and walking around with a flashlight. Despite his protests, she put him in her car and took him to a hospital. He'd taken "little pink pills," he told her.

She and a friend of Kelly's, Carlo Buonavolanto, tried to convince Kelly to go into the hospital for help, according to a police report. Kelly was groggy but seemed like he was improving. He convinced the two to take him home for the night. First, the group went back to the lumberyard in an attempt to look for the pills Kelly had taken. Flores-Buhelos found bottles of Aleve and Tylenol Cold, along with more damning evidence: she later told police she could smell exhaust. Kelly explained he had a truck running outside with a hose leading from its exhaust pipe into the trailer.

Flores-Buhelos and Buonavolanto turned off the truck and took Kelly back to Flores-Buhelos's condo. There, Flores-Buhelos found additional troubling evidence: a note he had left between her pillows, which she stuck in a drawer without reading. She told police she "knew" what it would say. Kelly promised Flores-Buhelos he'd never do anything like that again.

On Friday, September 11, after Kelly met with his lawyer about getting help for depression, and after he visited Walmart and texted Clarissa "I love 46," Flores-Buhelos sent Kelly a text with her work schedule to try to figure out a time for the two to have dinner. He didn't respond.

She tried again at 9:52 p.m., saying she was leaving work soon.

The response she finally received immediately spelled trouble. At 10:15 p.m. Kelly texted her, "come get me asap yard." While driving there, Flores-Buhelos got Kelly on the phone. He sounded groggy. She tried to keep him on the line, telling him repeatedly she was almost there. When she got there, she found Kelly slumped over the wheel of his Cadillac Escalade, covered in vomit. She put him in the backseat and drove to Oak Forest Hospital, while Kelly repeatedly asked her to slow down because he felt sick.

He told her what he'd taken: aspirin, Tylenol, and rat poison. A police officer came to the hospital and interviewed Kelly—the officer later described Kelly as combative and defensive. Kelly apparently told the officer he took Tylenol for pain after a recent surgery. Doctors eventually decided to transfer Kelly to Stroger Hospital, where the county's top toxicologist was on duty.

A friend took Flores-Buhelos back to the lumberyard to get her car, with Buonavolanto following. On the way, she called Mike Allen, a friend of Kelly's going back to their time at the University of Illinois. Allen headed to Stroger, too. The three were in the waiting room when hospital staff asked them if any of Kelly's family members were present. Allen later told police he knew then the outlook wasn't good. Allen called Kelly's wife, Carmen.

Kelly was pronounced dead at Stroger Hospital at 10:46 a.m. that morning. Allen, Flores-Buhelos, Buonavolanto, Carmen, and Kelly's sister Gertrude stayed with Kelly's body for two hours, when they were told it had to be moved to the medical examiner's office. The examiner later determined Kelly died of an aspirin and acetaminophen overdose. Allen offered to go back to Oak Forest to get Kelly's car, and on the way he stopped at the yard to the trailer to see if Kelly had left a note there. Instead, Allen found a Walmart bag with pills and opened boxes of rat poison. Police later reported seeing vomit and scattered poison pellets both inside and outside the trailer.

When he stepped inside, Allen found a sleeping bag on the floor, surrounded by pictures of Kelly's daughters and an empty gallon of milk. He sat on the steps outside the trailer for a while. When he left he took evidence of the poison and pills with him. He didn't want Kelly's family to see it.

News of the suicide drew sharp criticism of the techniques used by the feds working under Fitzgerald. The insurmountable pressure of three indictments, combined with the threat of being thrown in jail, must have been unbearable for Kelly.

"We kind of lose sight we're dealing with human beings, and people's lives are in the balance," said Larry Beaumont, a defense lawyer and one-time federal prosecutor who represented a potential witness against Kelly in the O'Hare contracts case. "Obviously, the government was playing hardball with him because he pled and then he was re-indicted. But by the same token, they had a job to do. I know that [the federal prosecutor] is a good person, and I'm sure is very upset by the outcome here."

News of the suicide spread through the ranks of law enforcement like wildfire. The possibility that Kelly could have been a witness in the Blagojevich case took the investigation into Kelly's death in a different direction. There were questions about who visited Kelly in the hospital, and about a mysterious car that was parked nearby. Based on what Kelly told the officer, police were "fairly certain" he tried to kill himself, Country Club Hills Mayor Dwight Welch said at a news conference. But an investigation into Kelly's final interactions with others was needed nonetheless. It was at this news conference that Welch did something odd—he held up for the news media a copy of Flores-Buhelos's driver's license, saying she was "lawyered up" and not cooperating.

This enraged Flores-Buhelos's lawyer.

"The mayor's a jackass," said Terry Gillespie, who doesn't take long to get red-faced. "You can print that." Flores-Buhelos met with investigators the following day. When she talked to police, she relayed one of her final interactions with Kelly. She told them that when medics began to move Kelly from one hospital to the next, he grew combative, and Flores-Buhelos tried to calm him.

"No, C," Flores-Buhelos said Kelly told her. "It's my life. Tell them they won. Tell them they won."

Christopher G. Kelly's funeral was held at St. John of the Cross Parish in Western Springs. The sun shone that day; the parking lot was filled with cars. Kelly's brother, Charlie, once a federal prosecutor, gave the eulogy. Rod and Patti Blagojevich showed up at the funeral. Patti grew emotional, at one point wiping away tears. When Rod, who had been on a coast-to-coast tour promoting *The Governor*, was on his way out of the church, a reporter called out to him. He rolled his eyes in response.

Chicago Alderman Ed Burke and Kelly's lawyers were there, too. In his eulogy, Charlie said that the entire Kelly family was proud of his brother. Charlie revealed that hours before his brother's death, Kelly had called him. Kelly had asked him to keep the eulogy brief and the funeral short.

His brother complied.

"Christopher Kelly is at peace," Charles Kelly told the crowd. "Nothing more. Nothing less."

Chapter Eight

The Tombstone Senator

However much the Washington, D.C., political establishment hoped Rod Blagojevich would resign or just fade away as quickly as possible, it wasn't going to happen. In the weeks following his arrest, Blagojevich continued to push the buttons of the political "lynch mob" that called for his ouster.

On December 30, 2008, Dave McKinney, Springfield bureau chief for the *Sun-Times*, was ringing the news desk with a breaking scoop. Going against every political recommendation, Blagojevich had rocked the political establishment: notwithstanding the charge that he had tried to sell the seat, he was going to name the senator to succeed Obama anyway.

It was going to be former Illinois Attorney General and one-time gubernatorial primary foe Roland Burris. Burris referred to himself in the third person and, most notably, already had a tombstone on which he had inscribed his various accomplishments. It read: "Trail Blazer...First African American in Illinois to become..." The posts of state attorney general and Illinois comptroller were also listed, but Burris left the top line open for what he was hoping would be a loftier political office.

Keeping future jurors in mind, Blagojevich's lawyers had helped steer the decision to pick his own senator before his ouster. The aim was to allow Blagojevich to say that he ended up choosing someone without any taint. Sam Adam Jr., who knew Roland Burris's son, Roland Jr., ended up approaching the Burrises with the idea. He had already approached another potential appointee before that: U.S. Rep. Danny Davis, an African American representing a Chicago district.

"I indicated I came to the conclusion there was too much discomfort on my part and the part of my family," Davis told *Sun-Times* Washington Bureau Chief Lynn Sweet. "It would be difficult to generate the trust level people would have to have in me. I just decided there was too much turmoil, too much disagreement. It was something I wanted to do, but I said I would not take an appointment from the governor."

When Blagojevich announced Burris's appointment, U.S. Rep. Bobby Rush, another African American representing a Chicago district, appeared at the news conference and endorsed the move. He used racially charged language, saying people shouldn't "hang or lynch the appointee, as you try to castigate the appointer."

Blagojevich liked the Burris appointment because Burris hadn't come up anywhere in the criminal complaint that had been so publicized by that point.

At a news conference, Blagojevich said, "As governor, I'm required to make this appointment." But the Washington establishment was outraged. Democratic Senate leaders including Senate Majority Leader Harry Reid and Dick Durbin together issued a statement denouncing Blagojevich's move.

"It is truly regrettable that despite requests from all 50 Democratic senators and public officials throughout Illinois, Governor Blagojevich would take the imprudent step of appointing someone to the United States Senate who would serve under a shadow and be plagued by questions of impropriety," the statement read. "We say this without prejudice toward Roland Burris's ability, and we respect his years of public service. But this is not about Mr. Burris; it is about the integrity of a governor accused of attempting to sell this United States Senate seat. Under these circumstances, anyone appointed by Governor Blagojevich cannot be an effective representative of the people of Illinois and, as we have said, will not be seated by the Democratic Caucus."

The showdown was on. The conflict launched a national constitutional debate as to whether an appointee meeting the basic qualifications to serve could be denied entry to the U.S. Senate. Burris, who would now be the only African American serving in the Senate, wasn't going to back down. He went to Washington to be sworn in.

On a rainy day in January 2009, Burris, carrying his certificate of appointment, headed to Capitol Hill along with a cadre of reporters. He was turned away. Senators insisted he couldn't be seated because of the taint remaining from Blagojevich's appointment. Illinois Secretary of State Jesse White had refused to sign papers certifying Blagojevich's appointment.

"My name is Roland Burris, the junior senator from the state of Illinois," Burris told reporters on Capitol Hill. "I was advised that my credentials were not in order." Burris mounted a legal challenge. Ultimately, the Senate leaders relented. They told Burris he would be seated, but with two caveats: first, that White must certify his appointment; and second, that Burris must testify in Springfield before a panel of Illinois lawmakers investigating Blagojevich. If Burris's testimony revealed no impropriety regarding his appointment, they said, he would be seated.

Sitting next to his attorney, Burris testified before the investigative panel on January 8, 2009. Burris was asked to list the members of Blagojevich's camp with whom he had discussions before his appointment, and detail the nature of those discussions. Jim Durkin, a Republican, asked Burris specifically if he had contact with six particular Blagojevich insiders: Rob Blagojevich, Doug Scofield, Bob Greenlee, John Wyma, Lon Monk, and John Harris.

Burris stopped to consult with his lawyer and then said, "I talked to some friends about my desire to be appointed, yes."

Durkin continued, "I guess the point is I was [sic] trying to ask: Did you speak to anybody who was on the governor's staff prior to the governor's arrest or anybody, any of those individuals or anybody who was closely related to the governor?"

Burris specifically mentioned Monk, the governor's ex-chief of staff, and no one else. On January 15, Burris was sworn in.

In the meantime, the *Sun-Times* obtained internal documents pertaining to Rod Blagojevich's campaign fund. Among them was a list seized by the feds that detailed fundraising targets. On the long list of donors was the name of a recently appointed U.S. senator: beside Burris's name were notations indicating that he'd had contact with the Friends of Blagojevich campaign committee, a "target amount" of $10,000, and the fact that Burris had left messages at the fundraising office. The documents indicated that Burris had discussions with Rob Blagojevich, specifically, and that the dates involved were within the time frame that federal authorities had wiretaps up and running.

When Burris's campaign was confronted with the newspaper's findings and reminded that federal wiretaps were up, it revealed a whopper: after Burris was seated by the Senate, he had quietly filed an affidavit adding to his testimony before the investigative panel. The problem was that some of the key members of the panel— including Durkin—had no idea about this filing. The affidavit, first made public in the *Sun-Times* story, made it clear that Burris discussed the Senate appointment with four Blagojevich insiders, including Rob, who headed the campaign fund.

"There were several facts that I was not given the opportunity to make [sic] during my testimony to the impeachment committee, so, upon receiving the transcripts, I voluntarily submitted an affidavit so everything was transparent," Burris said in a statement to the *Sun-Times*. On February 14, the *Sun-Times* reported that Burris gave varying statements under oath regarding his contacts with Blagojevich's camp and did not reveal substantive fundraising discussions with the ex-governor's brother until after he was sworn in as senator. In response to questions by the newspaper, Burris revealed he mailed the investigative panel a February 4 affidavit to supplement his testimony. Burris told the *Sun-Times* that Rob Blagojevich had asked him for a donation, but Burris "made it unequivocally clear…that it would be inappropriate and pose a major conflict because I was interested in the Senate vacancy."

The revelation exploded across the country. Incensed Republicans accused Burris of lying to the committee under oath and called for a perjury investigation, which was taken up by a Downstate prosecutor. A day after the report was published online, Burris held a nationally televised news conference in which he said, "I've always conducted myself with honor." The next day, the *Sun-Times* revealed the feds had been in contact with Burris about sitting for an interview during the Blagojevich investigation. Burris denied that this contact had been his motivation for amending his sworn testimony with the affidavit. The U.S. Senate launched an ethics probe while numerous politicians, as well as the *Sun-Times* and *Tribune*, called for Burris to resign. President Obama didn't outright ask for a resignation but sent a message that Burris carefully consider his future. The FBI interviewed Burris on a Saturday at his lawyer's office, ostensibly to keep the exchange out of the limelight. There, he was played an audio recording of a secretly taped phone call between himself and Rob Blagojevich.

When Blagojevich was indicted the following April, Burris reacted in a news statement, taking shots at the politicians who called for his ouster.

"To Blagojevich's credit, he decided as a final act it was important to appoint someone with an exceptional reputation of integrity and superior public service to the U.S. Senate seat," Burris said of himself. "Blagojevich gave Illinois the chance to accomplish three worthy goals—save the taxpayers an expensive special election, give the state a representative of proven experience, and show the rest of the world Illinois has good officials to take us beyond our tainted image."

That May, U.S. District Judge James Holderman allowed the public release of the audio recording, causing another headache for Burris. "God knows number one, I, I want to help Rod," Burris said on the recording. "Number two, I also wanna, you know, hope I get a consideration to get that appointment." Burris ended the call with a promise that he would write a check to Blagojevich before December 15, 2008. Blagojevich was arrested December 9. Burris never made the contribution and later claimed he never intended to make it.

A month later, Sangamon County State's Attorney John Schmidt ultimately declined to pursue perjury charges, saying some of Burris's statements were vague but wouldn't support a perjury charge. Burris blamed his situation on "muckraking" journalists who painted an unfair portrait of what had transpired. Burris said he had never been a contender for the Senate seat, so the fact that he had talked with Rob Blagojevich didn't matter.

In late 2009, the Senate ethics committee came out with a letter of admonition, which read: "The committee found that you should have known that you were providing incorrect, inconsistent, misleading, or incomplete information to the public, the

Senate, and those conducting legitimate inquiries into your appointment to the Senate."

The committee found that the November 13, 2008 phone call with Rob Blagojevich didn't rise to the level of an "explicit quid pro quo," but was "inappropriate." In the conversation, Burris is heard repeatedly bringing up the Senate seat appointment even as Rob Blagojevich tells him one has nothing to do with the other. Burris then says he may get a third party to donate on his behalf.

The committee found that even though the events happened before he was appointed to the Senate seat, they were "inextricably linked to your appointment," and therefore fell within the jurisdictions of the committee. "You should have known that any conversations you had about your desire to seek the Senate seat and about any possible fundraising for the Governor were critical to these inquiries," the letter continued.

According to Burris, the committee's letter meant that the Senate had cleared him.

The Blagojevich cloud hung over Burris for the entirety of his tenure in the U.S. Senate, which ran until 2010. Unable to raise money, Burris announced he would not attempt to run for another term.

Chapter Nine

Waging an Anti-Conviction Campaign

By late 2009, Blagojevich-related news saturated the airwaves. It seemed the public perception of his case was changing. He had come a long way from the days of being holed up in his Northwest Side house.

Blagojevich had been the populist governor for a reason. He knew how to talk off the cuff, and he knew how to appeal to people—especially in short sound bites. More of the public began to question the government's case. Many appeared to see Blagojevich as soft-headed—someone who talked nonsense on the phone, rather than a conniving politician.

Rod and Patti were increasingly strapped for cash, even with the $20,000 advance Blagojevich was given to write his book. As word spread that Alderman Mell was helping out his daughter financially, Patti took matters into her own hands.

After Zagel denied Blagojevich's petition to go to Costa Rica and appear on *I'm a Celebrity…Get Me Out of Here!*, Patti appeared in his stead. She traveled to the jungle, at one point got washed down a river, and, most famously, ate a tarantula on TV. She also had softer moments where she cried and talked about her husband's predicament.

Contrasted with the likes of the washed-out celebrities who were her castmates, Patti came off as down to earth and empathetic.

"It was probably the worst...the worst six months of our lives," Patti Blagojevich said on national TV. Reality stars Heidi Montag and Spencer Pratt, the quintessential couple famous for being famous, formed a circle with Patti, holding hands and saying a prayer. Pratt declared he would have voted for Blagojevich for governor.

"I look at them as the Heidi-Spencer of politics," he said at one point.

Insiders said that shows like the reality TV series were the means for Blagojevich's publicist, Glenn Selig, to get paid. As the architect of the media campaign, he would get a portion of the booking fees. As for Blagojevich, it appeared that talking was feeling better and better to the former governor. Now, instead of dodging small-time reporters in his hometown, he was getting flown first class to New York and treated just a little bit more like what he had always wanted to be—a celebrity.

With each major media appearance Blagojevich made that winter and spring, the whole situation seemed to grow more surreal. Each host had his or her own way of dealing with him. On *The View*, Blagojevich got his hair tousled. One of the most painful and embarrassing episodes occurred on one of his earliest bookings, *The Late Show with David Letterman*.

Blagojevich looked a bit nervous as he settled into the seat across from the late-night funnyman.

"Why exactly are you here, honest to God?" Letterman asked him.

"I've been wanting to be on your show in the worst way for the longest time," Blagojevich answered.

"Well, you're on in the worst way, believe me," Letterman said, to roaring laughter.

Letterman then told the ex-governor that as he listened to him profess his innocence on the air, he was struck.

"The more you talked and the more you repeated your innocence, the more I thought, 'Oh, this guy's guilty.'"

The exchange was beyond awkward, with Letterman openly mocking the ex-governor and Blagojevich knowing it, and taking it. Letterman played an audio cut of Blagojevich talking to Rob about a contribution from track owner Johnny Johnston. The conversation was an FBI-recorded call that was used in the impeachment proceeding against Blagojevich.

In a later series of interviews tied to the start of his impeachment trial in Springfield, Blagojevich seemed to offend someone new every day, comparing himself to Martin Luther King, Mahatma Gandhi, Winston Churchill, Abraham Lincoln, and Nelson Mandela, among others. Blagojevich told MSNBC's Rachel Maddow that he absolutely would testify at his trial.

"Now I'm not just here talking the talk, I'm gonna walk the walk, which is right up to the witness stand. And when I take the stand and I testify and I swear on the Holy Bible to tell the truth, I expect, and far more importantly than that, I think, the people of Illinois expect and they deserve that the government does the same."

Blagojevich would often lapse into campaign-speak, touting his main causes in office. Awestruck by the spectacle of a criminally charged governor actually talking about his case on national TV, the media and the public alike ate up the interviews, at least initially.

Blagojevich ultimately even launched his own radio show on Chicago talk-radio station WLS-AM. (This was a controversial move on the station's part, to say the least. The manager who supported the idea at WLS was eventually let go.) When Blagojevich published his book, *The Governor*, it became the occasion for another New York media tour. All the while, he embraced his role as national punch line. He commonly used self-deprecating humor in his appearances. When the Second City comedy troupe mounted its mocking *Rod Blagojevich Superstar* revue, Blagojevich showed up one night and won a standing ovation.

Throughout the media frenzy, he tried to portray himself as the little guy up against a government that had overstepped by invading his home to make secret recordings of private conversations. Using his populist appeal, Blagojevich worked hard to spin the most damning evidence against him, attempting to argue that it wasn't damning at all. He dared his prosecutors repeatedly to play not just some of the recordings they'd made, but all of them. What was on the tapes, he'd say again and again, was just talk, and it was legal. As time wore on, Blagojevich developed a mantra: "Play all the tapes." It would be repeated throughout the time leading up to his trial.

The bold, extravagant public persona that Blagojevich developed after he was charged was far different from the man his aides described working for as governor. Some told stories of a governor who hid in the bathroom to avoid conversations with the state's budget director. They spoke of a man who had to be tracked down at dinner to veto legislation that would otherwise turn into law. They cited his pettiness: once, Blagojevich fired the wife of Madigan's chief of staff, despite the fact that she'd worked for the state for 24 years with a clean record. They told how Blagojevich, an Elvis lover, would pitch a fit if they couldn't supply his favorite Paul Mitchell hairbrush. Blagojevich, long known to be obsessed with his bushy black pompadour, called the brush the "football," which was a reference to the so-called "nuclear football," the briefcase that the president carries at all times that holds the codes for the U.S. nuclear arsenal.

As a politician, Blagojevich was a big-picture type. He focused on populist issues like children's healthcare, prescription drugs, and flu shots. He thrived on playing to the cameras, politicking, and connecting with average people. In a 2004 column for the *Sun-Times*, Carol Marin noted that many state lawmakers complained that Blagojevich was distant. He stuck to promoting his own populist issues and didn't return their calls. He didn't appear to put much effort into trying to forge partnerships.

"What really makes their blood boil is that this hands-off approach is paying off for the governor. Politicians and reporters may watch this internecine warfare like it's HBO, but the public, much of it, couldn't care less," Marin wrote. "And so Blagojevich, who undoubtedly sees the White House somewhere on his horizon, has maintained his popularity with the voting public. In spite of some erosion Downstate, legislative polls taken this fall show his numbers surging in the suburbs among both Democrats and Republicans. Positioning yourself as an anti-Springfield, anti-Madigan, anti-Daley guy apparently has its rewards." However, as Marin also noted, political fortunes "can turn on a dime."

Blagojevich ran his anti-conviction campaign much the same way. He didn't engage the main legal players but went around them, arguing his case in the media. Blagojevich didn't get into the nitty-gritty of the charges against him while arguing his case in public. He stuck to simple sound bites and was often intentionally misleading. He waged war against the chief prosecutor, against all the prosecutors in the trial. "Play all the tapes" remained his rallying cry.

In letters from a series of former Blagojevich aides to Judge Zagel that were obtained by *Sun-Times* reporter Dan Mihalopoulos, former Blagojevich top aide Clayton Harris III (no relation to

John Harris) said Blagojevich once directed him to fire the entire legal department.

"They lacked the professionalism that the governor believed should have been exhibited," Harris wrote. He said Blagojevich ordered him to hire an unemployed lawyer "he met in line at Starbucks to be chief legal counsel of the state of Illinois!"

Harris also told of a practice that many of Blagojevich's aides spoke of: how the governor would make a crazed directive and they would respond by ignoring it. If Blagojevich asked, they would lead him to believe they had done as he told them. Eventually, Blagojevich would move on and forget about it, they'd say.

In another letter, Larry Trent, former director Illinois State Police, told of a bizarre proposal by the governor: Blagojevich offered then-Mayor Daley state troopers and helicopters from the National Guard to help clean up the city's streets. Trent said Blagojevich "wanted to ride with the group" of state troopers—which he nicknamed "The Rough Riders"—into violence-torn parts of the city. Blagojevich, a fan of old Westerns, also wanted to outfit the new force with "some special, provocative, and recognizable apparel," Mihalopoulos wrote. It was perhaps more than appropriate, then, that in the summer of the year when Blagojevich made that proposal, the *Sun-Times* superimposed Blagojevich's face onto an old Western movie shot of John Wayne and put it on its front page with the headline, "Sheriff Rod to Mayor Daley: 'I'LL CLEAN UP THIS TOWN, PARDNER.'"

Phone logs from the governor's office showed that Blagojevich called the newspaper's publisher the next day to discuss the front page.

If Blagojevich reveled in his exposure doing the media circuit, he kept getting disrupted by reality. After prosecutors filed an explosive proffer—a roadmap of their case—negative headlines pounded the Blagojevich camp.

The court document included allegations that the Blagojeviches actually got illicit money through their connections. And they said it came from Tony Rezko.

Rezko, they said, gave Blagojevich's wife, Patti, nearly $100,000 under the guise that she was doing real estate work. Newspapers had been asking questions about Patti's real estate work even before the charges. When the governor was challenged about the legitimacy of Patti's work for Rezko's companies, he shot back that it was "Neanderthal" to suggest she didn't do her own work. The suggestion, he complained, was an insult to working women.

In October 2008, reporters caught up with the governor after the dedication of Chicago State University's Emil and Patricia Jones Convocation Center. They asked him about a recent *Sun-Times* report that the FBI had questioned contractors who worked on a $90,000 rehab of his home in 2003 that had been overseen by a Rezko company. Blagojevich shrugged it off.

"Much ado about nothing," he said. "The home renovation that we did, Patti and I paid for personally." The governor had already refused the newspaper's request to release contractor invoices, canceled personal checks, or other documents to back up that claim.

"The canceled checks are where they belong. They're at the bank," he said. Federal prosecutors thought differently. They would later craft an indictment that included charges involving Rezko's work on the Blagojevich home.

It was true that the Blagojeviches paid the money from their own account. But this is how the feds traced the money. Prosecutors said that developers offered Rezko, who headed the real estate company Rezmar, the opportunity to be a broker on his purchase of two condo units. Rezko wanted the brokerage fee directed to Patti Blagojevich even though she'd played no role in the deal, prosecutors alleged. The two developers wouldn't do it.

A check for the brokerage fee was written to Patti's real estate business, but "that check was sent back to the title company with instructions that the check be issued to" Rezmar, the indictment said. Eventually, on January 21, 2004, Rezmar got a $40,000 check for a brokerage fee. The next day, Rezmar issued a check to Patti—for $40,000. On January 23, Patti deposited the check into her real estate business's bank account. She then took $40,000 out of that account and put it into her personal checking account. The following day, according to prosecutors, Patti paid vendors who did work on her home. And, like her husband had said, it was paid out of their personal checking account. The amount paid was just less than $40,000.

A week after the proffer's release, Blagojevich responded the way he knew best: he held a news conference. Blagojevich, wearing a bit of makeup, made his remarks at 5:03 p.m.—just in time for three TV networks to carry them live. He called prosecutors "cowards" and "liars" and then turned and took no questions from reporters. In doing so, he was targeting potential jurors, former federal prosecutor Dean Polales said at the time.

"He's trying to communicate to the potential jury pool that he truly believes in his own innocence," Polales said. Privately, those in the government challenged reporters, asking them why they just showed up and allowed Blagojevich to say what he wanted if he wasn't going to allow himself to be challenged.

In his blustery, two-minute address, a finger-waving Blagojevich summoned Fitzgerald to show up in the federal courthouse the next day at high noon.

"They're now hitting below the belt and attacking my wife. They are cowards, and they are liars," he said. "Patti is a devoted mother. She's a loving wife. She's a licensed professional. I challenge Mr. Fitzgerald. Why don't you show up in court tomorrow and explain to everybody, say to the whole world, why you don't want those tapes that you made played in court," Blagojevich said. "I'll be in court tomorrow, I hope you're man enough to be there tomorrow, too." Blagojevich accused the government of trying to sneak into court to block him from playing all the recordings at his trial. But this was spin and Blagojevich knew it. Judge Zagel had ruled against all the tapes being played. Zagel did, though, tell Blagojevich's lawyers that if the former governor took the stand, he likely would be allowed to play most recordings he chose to play.

The next day, Blagojevich showed up to court. Fitzgerald did not. And Blagojevich said nothing in the courtroom. He did listen, however. Zagel broke it down, explaining in a calm voice that it was he, and not the government, who would decide which tapes would be played in court.

In the thick of the media blitz, a man with a golden finger tapped Blagojevich on the shoulder. Donald Trump, someone who had crossed paths with the former governor years earlier, invited Blagojevich to appear on *Celebrity Apprentice*. The show gave him yet another national platform. It ended with his getting "fired" early on, while exposing his calamitous relationship with technology. To the shock of many, Blagojevich revealed he couldn't type, text, or use email.

"There's a whole lot of technology that's passed me by," he said. After he was booted, he appeared on *The Ellen Degeneres Show* and announced he had since learned how to send text messages. Nonetheless, with *Celebrity Apprentice*, Blagojevich had gotten still more free national airtime to talk about his case. He painted himself as the anti-establishment underdog, a fighter who would take on the U.S. Attorney and his team of prosecutors.

"I think when all this happened, people thought that he was a crook and had done something terrible," Selig said. "I think that now people have come to understand this is a man who is fighting for his career and his life right now, insisting from day one that he didn't do these things."

Blagojevich and Selig made a major misstep, though. In January 2010, an *Esquire* magazine article quoted Blagojevich proclaiming himself to be "blacker than Barack Obama." He elaborated: "I shined shoes. I grew up in a five-room apartment." He quickly called a news conference to recant, saying, "What I said was stupid, stupid, stupid." "Blacker than Obama" was, for a time, the most searched Google term associated with "Blagojevich."

Just before trial, in what many saw as the height of irony, Blagojevich spoke to a standing-room-only crowd at Northwestern University about ethics, poking fun at himself along the way. He was booed when he likened U.S. Senate leaders to southern segregationists for initially not allowing Roland Burris into the U.S. Capitol in 2009.

"Shame!" someone from the crowd shouted.

"You don't like Burris?" Blagojevich asked.

"No—you," the shouter responded.

"My friend, I have love in my heart for you," Blagojevich replied.

One student asked Blagojevich why, if he were innocent, he had gone on a media "circus" tour.

"If I did things wrong, I would do none of that," Blagojevich said. "It ain't so. I didn't do it. And by the way, play all the tapes."

One student, Samir Pendse, said Blagojevich left him with "a sleazy feel." But the more Blagojevich talked, the more the Northwestern senior couldn't help but feel some empathy for him.

"It was such self-deprecating stuff, you almost at times had to empathize with him," Pendse said.

Ravi Umarji, also a senior, said that while he was skeptical of Blagojevich's claims of innocence, he was surprised to find himself at times laughing with him—not just at him. "The key thing I came away with: I'm shocked by how good of a speaker he is," Umarji said. "I was amazed by how well he can get a crowd to respond to him."

As the governor's trial neared, there was much speculation about whether Rezko would be called to the witness stand. Though sources privately said that the government would never do it, the defense believed it could be a possibility. In a filing made just before the trial, defense lawyers had sought to get a copy of the FBI interview involving Obama. Zagel upheld the federal authorities' refusal to release it, saying it wasn't relevant to the case. The defense lawyers also suggested they would try to subpoena Obama, even for a televised interview. Trying to make their case for doing so, they filed a lengthy memo, much of which was blacked out.

They filed it electronically, though, and said they didn't realize that all of the blacked-out portions were completely readable when one just copied and pasted the relevant sections.

In the memo, which soon went viral, defense lawyers stated that Rezko said he "believed he transmitted a quid pro quo offer from a lobbyist to the public official, whereby the lobbyist would hold a fundraiser for the official in exchange for favorable official action, but that the public official rejected the offer." It also said the public official "denies any such conversation." While the memo didn't name Obama as the "public official," it was pretty clear the president was the official referred to, given another passage in the filing that said Obama "is the only one who can testify as to the veracity" of Rezko's allegations.

When this matter went public, Zagel blew his top in a private exchange with the lawyers. What the defense memo revealed was some of the most sensitive material that had been under seal. Blagojevich's lawyers said that the failure to properly black out portions of the memo was an inadvertent error.

Outside the courtroom during a hearing held before the trial, Sam Adam Jr. chatted with reporters. How did he feel about Blagojevich's media blitz? he was asked. Most lawyers urge their clients not to make public statements about their cases.

"I'm all for it," Adam said, breaking into a broad smile. Adam brimmed with enthusiasm. "We're going to make him into a superstar." Raising his finger for emphasis, he added, "And no one wants to convict a superstar."

Sam Adam Jr.'s finger-wagging, preacher-style persona had made him a legend in the dingy 26th and California Streets state courthouse. He was charming, self-deprecating, and funny. A storyteller, he had perfected a facial expression that simultaneously conveyed both shock and outrage. He had been part of the team that defended R&B singer R. Kelly against charges that he'd had sex with an underaged girl. In the Kelly case, there was videotaped evidence but no victim, as the girl involved would not testify. As a result, the jury acquitted Kelly.

Ed Genson had led Kelly's team. Genson had seen the Kelly trial as an opportunity for Sam Adam Jr. and had given him the limelight—he let the younger Adam give both the defense's opening statement and closing arguments. One reporter covering the case said Adam Jr.'s closing argument was so riveting that when it concluded, he fought the urge to rise to his feet and applaud.

Before Blagojevich's first trial, in state court, Adam Jr.'s record was 60-5 in cases where he gave both the opening and closing statements. That included winning the acquittal of a man who had stabbed someone 61 times. But Adam Jr. and his father were aware they lacked experience in the federal arena. It had a more staid style. It drew different jury pools. It saw more one-sided victories. In state court, the government wins cases about 50 or 60 percent of the time. In federal court, prosecutors nearly never lose. Their success rate is 95 percent.

The fact that the experienced Ed Genson had left the Blagojevich defense team was also an issue. Genson, who was in Springfield fighting the impeachment efforts, had said he felt increasingly isolated from the remainder of the legal team. Though Genson and Sam Adam Sr. were longtime friends and had worked together for decades, it was clear that Genson felt he was getting shut out of the decision making about Blagojevich. He announced that he was resigning from Blagojevich's defense team.

The last nail in the coffin, though, came after, with an incident that called back a conflict between Blagojevich and Mayor Daley.

In September 2008, just before the wiretaps went up, Mayor Daley publicly humiliated Blagojevich by answering a question about the governor in a high-pitched voice, declaring Blagojevich "cuckoo."

Later, after he was charged and faced ouster by the legislature, Blagojevich declared that his impeachment trial was fixed. He theorized about why the legislature wanted him gone, saying they planned to ram through a tax increase that he wouldn't have allowed. When reporters took the claim to Daley, he echoed his sentiment from months earlier.

"I'll say it again: cuckoo!"

Sam Adam Sr. echoed this exchange in his response to reporters when asked about why Genson quit the Blagojevich defense team.

"Cuckoo!" Adam said, pointing to his head.

That solidified it. Genson, who had brought the team together for Blagojevich, would not return. The relationship with the elder Adam was never repaired.

Adam Jr. looked confident as he strode in and out of court. But in one-on-one coversations, there was a hint of insecurity behind his eyes. He knew he had built a reputation high on showmanship, but was he cut out for this? This was federal court. He was going up against the feared Patrick Fitzgerald. He knew there were many who doubted him.

Before the trial, Adam said the defense team's best weapon was the government's view of him.

"We're a joke," he said. "They think I'm a clown." Before opening statements, Adam practiced his remarks in front of his colleagues. The government, they thought, didn't know what was coming.

Chapter Ten

A Governor Goes to Trial

S ix years after the investigation began, 18 months after his arrest, and 17 months after the launch of his infamous national media blitz, the day had finally arrived. On June 3, 2010, Rod Blagojevich and his brother Rob would arrive in federal court to face extensive corruption charges. Jury selection began that morning, with attorneys whittling down a group of 100 potential jurors.

The U.S. Marshals used yellow tape to cordon off an area for Blagojevich to walk into the federal building and, presumably, to keep the media from trampling one another. It looked more crime scene than red carpet. There were some people from the public, holding cell phones and awaiting the ex-governor's arrival. One was carrying a homemade sign, white poster board with black writing: "If a man can't talk crap in his own home, then take my husband please!"

Another woman was holding a sign that read: "Rod's not cuckoo, Rod's not guilty."

The first Blagojevich to arrive was Rob.

"I expect to be vindicated," he said as a cadre of cameras pounced on him on his way into the courthouse.

"Great, I feel great," Rod Blagojevich said as he exited his car. He shook hands with and stopped to talk to supporters who were holding signs, causing some people to break through the security tape. After maneuvering through security, Patti calmly stopped in front of a phalanx of microphones and addressed reporters in the first-floor lobby. Clad in a black dress, black-and-white blazer, and black high heels, Mrs. Blagojevich talked about how her husband's arrest 18 months before had been a terrible day for her family.

"Today is a good day because today begins a process to correct a terrible injustice that's been done to my husband, our family, and the people of Illinois," she said. "My husband as governor did great things for people, and he continued to fight for them always. My husband is an honest man, and I know that he's innocent. Thank you."

Rod Blagojevich, wearing a blue suit and blue tie, smiled at the media throng and headed up to the courtroom.

The trial got underway amidst competing concerns about the jury pool. Blagojevich had done so much media that it may have tainted the jury pool. On the other hand, the feds' explosive criminal complaint, which outlined the embarrassing recordings, likely tainted the jury pool in another way.

The first day of jury selection was June 3, 2010. The former governor took notes, joked with his lawyers, and, at times, appeared to suppress laughter. Rob, who sat at the table behind Rod's, sighed deeply on a few occasions, seeming to grasp the gravity of what would unfold in the coming months. He had traveled to Chicago from Nashville the week prior and came to court with only his lawyers. The Blagojevich brothers walked in and out of the courtroom and the courthouse separately and did not interact all day. The first day of trial ended weeks of speculation over whether Blagojevich would cut a deal to save his brother from facing trial alongside him.

That first day, it turned out that each potential juror had already heard something about Blagojevich's case. One dismissed juror disclosed that people in the jury pool were reading and listening to news about the case. The judge reminded the panel to avoid all media reports, as difficult as it was. All but one juror said he or she could be fair in the courtroom. The jurors represented a broad swath of the public, including college students, people looking for work, a man who'd once served on an 18-month federal grand jury, a machinist, schoolteachers, and another man who said he had once testified as an expert witness. One woman said she did not trust "most politicians" but later said she could be fair in this case.

Judge Zagel queried the jurors with flair, chuckling over senior moments with a woman who said she struggled with memory loss, and posing a personal question to a hockey player.

"Do you have all your teeth?" he said to much laughter.

"Yes, I do," came the answer.

In particular, Zagel roasted a 22-year-old college graduate for, among other things, consulting with a lawyer about how to get out of jury duty and marking "yes" on his questionnaire about whether he had a medical condition. His illness: a bad temper. In concluding his questioning of this young man, Zagel asked, "Is there anything you wouldn't say to get out of jury service?" and alluded to the embarrassment he might suffer if his jury questionnaire was made public.

"The only thing that saves you from me not making this public," Zagel said, "is the fact we do destroy these questionnaires."

With opening statements in the trial just hours away, the Blagojevich team made a last-ditch filing to throw out the ex-governor's case, calling it an "improper criminalization of his rights under the First Amendment." The team knew the attempt would fail, but it once more aired out the notion that Blagojevich's "crimes" were all talk.

"In this case, the defendant was engaged in political speech and expression," his federal court filing said. "The government alleges that the political process in which he was engaged was criminal. This is a violation of the defendant's rights of freedom of speech and expression afforded him under the United States constitution."

Blagojevich's trial opened on a Tuesday. Spectators began lining up outside 219 S. Dearborn Street in Chicago, outside the federal courthouse, at 4:00 a.m. All of the courtroom tickets were dispensed by 7:30 a.m. When Rod Blagojevich arrived, he walked over to shake hands with a supporter who shouted, "I'm with you!"

"I fought for you the whole way," Blagojevich said. "I never let you down." Blagojevich then embraced legendary New York author Jimmy Breslin and walked in behind him, appearing to use him as a human shield as he approached the media pit. Blagojevich was calm and composed as he addressed reporters for about two minutes, standing next to Patti. He called the day "historic" and said the public and media had been "lied to."

"This is frankly a new beginning," he said. "Finally you'll be able to hear the things I've been dying to tell you...and it begins with opening statements."

As media, family, and reporters stuffed into the 25th-floor courtroom, Zagel took a moment to tell Blagojevich that there would be no tweeting from court. Blagojevich had been tweeting on and off since his arrest in December 2008, as had his publicist. Zagel added, "I do not want anybody in the well of the court using Twitter during trial."

The final jury of 12, plus 6 alternates, walked in. The group was made up of 11 women and 7 men. It included a math teacher, 2 college students, and 2 former Marines. Among them was James

Matsumoto, who was born in a Japanese internment camp in California and would later act as the jury's foreperson. Also on the panel was JoAnn Chiakulas, a quiet older woman in glasses who came to court with her hair done neatly every day. This retired state public health worker didn't register on the radar screen for either the prosecution or defense. Later, she would become well known: the surprising holdout who stuck to her guns in deliberations, despite intense pressure from fellow jurors.

The overflow room—a courtroom down the hall from the proceedings that had audio from the trial piped in—was packed full. "Shoulder to shoulder!" a court security officer shouted, telling people to slide closer together on the packed wooden benches.

The petite Assistant U.S. Attorney Carrie Hamilton, dressed in a dark suit and with her blonde hair up in a simple ponytail, had two giant water bottles at the ready. Finally, she was given the OK to begin.

"On the North Side of Chicago is a hospital named Children's Memorial Hospital. In 2008, Children's Memorial was trying to get a grant to treat sick kids," she said in a slow, clear voice. But before "defendant Blagojevich" would allow that grant, she said, he demanded something in return. "Now that he had decided to help the hospital, he wanted to make sure the hospital was going to help him. Blagojevich decided if the hospital president wasn't going to help him, he wasn't going to help the hospital. This was just one in a series of illegal shakedowns that started shortly after Rod Blagojevich became governor of Illinois in [2003] and continued until he was arrested in 2008."

Hamilton spoke steadily and deliberately, pausing to emphasize each point. She took jurors through the alleged schemes. Blagojevich used middlemen to operate his shakedowns, she said, and throughout his tenure as Illinois's chief executive he ruled with one question in mind: "What about me?" She spent just five minutes of the hour the prosecution team took for its opening statement speaking to the most sensational of charges: that Blagojevich tried to sell Obama's vacant Senate seat to the highest bidder.

For the first time, prosecutors revealed that Blagojevich had been about $200,000 in debt in the fall of 2008. Prosecutors charted out Blagojevich's finances on a big screen so jurors could see a link between his plummeting income and the indictments of key members of his inner circle. Hamilton said Blagojevich viewed the Senate seat appointment as "his answer to his career problems and financial troubles," as he had not yet decided whether to seek reelection in 2010.

"He had no career plans for what he was going to do and no plans of what he was going to do with this financial situation," she told the jury. "For Governor Blagojevich, his golden ticket arrived on November 4, 2008," she said. That's the day Barack Obama was elected president of the United States, giving Blagojevich sole rights to replace him in the Senate. Proof of all of this, she repeatedly stressed, was in the multitude of recordings obtained by the government.

Blagojevich bit his lip and stared up at Hamilton, but often buried his head in a yellow legal pad on which he wrote furiously. Sometimes it seemed he was forcing himself to write just to distract himself. Other times, he'd lose himself and stare right at Hamilton, looking like he wanted to explode.

Hamilton told jurors that they would hear conversations recorded from Blagojevich's home phone and from Rob Blagojevich's cell phone.

"What you are going to hear is these defendants talking about this corruption at the time it was happening, when they did not believe that anyone besides their trusted insiders were listening," she said. The crowd looked on, engaged.

Next up was Michael Ettinger, who said he had the honor of representing "retired Lieutenant Colonel Robert Blagojevich."

"I'm going to tell you now, I'm going to tell you until the end," Ettinger continued. "He's innocent. He's an innocent man and he's a great man. And I think at the end, when you've heard all the evidence, you're going to agree with me."

Ettinger walked the jury through Rob's life—being careful to call him "Robert" and not "Rob," which could be mistaken for "Rod."

"He's not a politician," Ettinger said. "He's a businessman." Ettinger stressed that when the two brothers were in college "they weren't close," and they continued to grow apart as adults. Robert had done his brother a favor by agreeing to help run the Friends of Blagojevich campaign fund, Ettinger said, and he did it legally.

"Robert followed the rules," Ettinger said. "Let me promise you, the evidence will show. Robert followed the rules." Ettinger set the stage for the jury to hear numerous phone calls from Robert by saying that when Robert was asked to call someone, he would call them three or four times because he was "persistent," not because he shook anyone down. Ettinger told the jury about the confusing back-and-forth between the brothers when it came to Blagojevich appointing a replacement for Obama's Senate seat.

"In the last ten days, Rod has changed his mind eight times!" Ettinger recalled. Rod Blagojevich and his group of attorneys, sitting at a separate table, knowingly chuckled at this comment. Ettinger said the tapes would show that his client repeatedly told donors their money had no influence on the Senate seat appointment.

Sam Adam Jr. came to the floor next and, by design, was nearly inaudible. The room grew quiet as he gestured toward his stomach.

Adam's remarks were something of a dramatic reenactment, beginning with a whisper.

"I know when you hear the government's opening you got a feeling," he said to the jury. "I know you get it in your gut, you know it. But by the end of this case, I'm telling you, that man there is as honest as the day is long," he said, his voice rising. "And you will know it where? In your gut!"

Adam spoke so loudly that his booming voice at times could be heard down the hall outside the courtroom. At other times, he dropped the volume so low that listeners strained to hear him. The defense lawyer poked at the government's case, accusing the "same people chasing Bin Laden" of mounting a mammoth case that alleged all sorts of money-making schemes against an honest man with no money. The government said Blagojevich's financial constraints gave him motive to shake people down and try cashing in on the Senate seat appointment. But Adam told jurors to look at it a different way.

"He's broke! He's broke!" Adam yelled. "You know why he's broke, ladies and gentlemen? It's not hard. He didn't take a dime!" Adam painted a picture of a governor unaware of the corruption swirling around in his administration because he was consumed by "big ideas," obsessed with not raising taxes on everyday Illinoisans, and fooled by his associates, who initially dazzled him only to ultimately let him down. Adam gave a new spin to the charges that Blagojevich wanted to appoint Jackson to the Senate seat in exchange for a $1.5-million campaign contribution: Blagojevich was just messing with the Washington, D.C., establishment. The ex-governor knew top Democrats didn't think Jackson was electable in 2010, so Blagojevich artificially propped Jackson up, hoping party leaders would panic and embark on a deal that would eventually force Michael Madigan to push through Blagojevich's legislative package, Adam said.

This plan worked, according to Adam: On December 8, 2008, Rahm Emanuel called Blagojevich's top aide, offering to approach Madigan about advancing Blagojevich's package in exchange for appointing Lisa Madigan to the seat. The then-governor was arrested the next day.

Adam mocked the Jacksons, causing one juror to lean forward in his seat, laughing. The scheme wasn't true, he declared, because, "Jesse Jackson ain't giving nobody any money." Adam strode back and forth, walking up to the witness stand, then back to the defense table. He spoke of Lon Monk, referring to him as the "California guy" with "beautiful hair." He then paused and looked at Blagojevich, rattling off a line that made more jurors laugh than most of the things Adam said over the course of the two hours he spoke: "Maybe not as good as others," he said of his shaggy-headed client.

Adam said Blagojevich, son of a working-class Serbian immigrant, saw something he'd never seen before on the Monk family front lawn: two peacocks. "He's kicking rats out his back door growing up, and this man has peacocks!" Adam shouted, drawing snickers. He briefly switched gears to the topic of Patti Blagojevich, and prepared the jury for what they were to hear out of the former First Lady's mouth. Patti was a "good woman," Adam said, one that "stands by her man." That explains why jurors would hear Patti say "Fuck the Cubs" on a recording. Of course she disliked the Cubs, he said—the team was owned by the Tribune Company, and that newspaper's editorial board wanted her husband out of office.

Hamilton had said that Tony Rezko had funneled $150,000 in sham real estate consulting fees and commissions to Patti in 2003 and 2004. Sitting in the front row, Patti muttered something unintelligible as Hamilton made the accusation. Later, Adam said the former First Lady earned every penny. "She did her job and she got her commission," he said.

The next day began with the FBI's point man on the stand. Special Agent Daniel Cain explained how the feds bugged the former governor's campaign office and then listened from a van outside. The FBI eventually tapped the phone lines. Cain testified that his office secretly recorded from 10 different phones or locations in the course of the Blagojevich probe. The recordings happened from October 22 through December 9, 2008—right up until the day Blagojevich was arrested.

The recordings included two bugs and eight wiretaps of cell phones and desk phones—including Blagojevich's cell and home phones, his brother Rob's cell phone, John Harris's cell and desk phones, and Lon Monk's cell phone. They also included both bugs and wiretaps in the campaign office. In all, 5,000 calls were recorded, and 1,100 of those were relevant to the case, Cain said. He then presented a disk of about 100 conversations that the government would play at trial.

That set things up for Lon Monk's testimony. Monk, Blagojevich's friend, roommate, groomsman, and running buddy, walked into the courtroom while Blagojevich, sitting at the defense table, stared right at him, following Monk with his eyes all the way to the witness stand. Monk seemed intent on looking straight ahead as he passed the defense table. When he got to the witness stand, Blagojevich leaned toward Sorosky and muttered something, looking irritated, shaking his head.

Prosecutor Christopher Niewoehner, who had taken the lead in the Rezko prosecution, asked Monk what the most important line was on a particular campaign finance form. The amount of contributions received, Monk answered.

"It showed political strength, it showed that the campaign was strong and well-run," Monk said.

Niewoehner asked why that would be a big deal.

"You could spend it on media and grassroots events....You could travel more than other candidates who didn't have as much money," Monk said. "It showed a likelihood that he [Blagojevich] would win." Monk then talked about how Blagojevich's two biggest fundraisers, Kelly and Rezko, raised millions of dollars, which immediately gave them the most influence over the governor's administration. Kelly and Rezko were part of the governor's transition team in 2003 and had control over dozens of crucial appointments in the Blagojevich administration, Monk said. Monk added that Blagojevich vacationed with Kelly and his family. They went to ball games and meals together. They spoke frequently, with Kelly doing the greatest share of the money-raising—millions of dollars between 2001 and 2004, Monk said.

Niewoehner asked Monk if, in his duties as Blagojevich's chief of staff in 2003 and 2004, he was asked to participate in "pay-to-play" politics.

When asked by Rezko and Harris, Monk said, he had helped arrange favors for campaign donors—"in some instances to get appointed to boards and commissions, and in some instances to get state business."

Blagojevich grew increasingly animated at the defense table. He shook his head and scribbled on his yellow notepad with vigor.

"At times would Rezko and Kelly ask you to do so something with respect to the individuals and firms?" Niewoehner asked. Monk said yes.

"What did you typically do?" the prosecutor asked.

Monk paused.

"Whatever they asked."

Monk spoke of how Blagojevich, Monk, Kelly, and Rezko referred to themselves as 1, 2, 3, and 4. They attended secret meetings where they discussed how to cash in on state action. He described a 2003 meeting in which he, Blagojevich, Rezko, and Kelly were all in the room talking about how to make money off state deals. He said one of Rezko's ideas involved creating an insurance agency that would make money by getting business from the state. Rezko led the discussion, writing on a blackboard nine different ideas that would make each of them money. Each idea was worth about $100,000, Monk said. Monk was asked: How was that money going to be divided? "Equally," he replied. "All told, hundreds of thousands of dollars...in total."

Monk said Blagojevich agreed not to take the money until after he was out of office, "because we didn't want anyone to know what was going on. There wouldn't be as much scrutiny....In all likelihood [it was] wrong and we would be breaking the law."

As Monk recounted this in court, Blagojevich appeared livid, shaking his head and shooting glances at him and the prosecutor.

Monk talked about a similar meeting that happened at the Beverly Wilshire Hotel in California after Blagojevich and his entourage traveled there in a private plane. In another part of testimony, Monk alleged that a $10-billion state deal was controlled not by experts in Blagojevich's administration, but fundraising friends who wanted to make money off the deal. The four of them were to win a $500,000 kickback off the deal, he said.

Monk said he listened intently when Kelly explained to him how they could profit from state deals.

"I was intrigued and I wanted to make money," he said.

While the money was paid into a secret account held by Rezko, Monk never testified whether he knew if Blagojevich ultimately got any of the money. Monk did say that in 2003, early in Blagojevich's first term in the governor's office, Blagojevich gave the OK to sell all $10 billion in bonds in one day—rather than over several days, and through several different firms. Handling the huge task was Bear Stearns, a firm recommended by Kelly and Rezko. Blagojevich gave the nod to the deal only after Kelly took him aside in a government meeting and told him what to do. Kelly was the only non-staffer present at the meeting, Monk said. Kelly later told Monk he pushed Blagojevich to approve the deal.

"It was either really going to help fundraising or we were going to make money...the four of us," Monk said Kelly explained.

Monk said the $10-billion deal was steered to Bear Stearns while Bob Kjellander was the firm's lobbyist. Monk said that as a reward for the business, Kjellander "had given Tony $500,000 and...Tony was putting that in a separate account for the four of us." Monk said he, Rezko, and others didn't want anyone to know about the account "because it would have been illegal." Kjellander was also a bigwig with the National Republican Committee at the time. Monk testified that Kelly later blew his top at Rezko for withdrawing $100,000 from the account.

"By withdrawing the money it would make the account more visible than it otherwise would [be] because there was activity in it," Monk said. Kelly told Rezko to put the money back in, Monk said. Kelly wasn't worried Rezko would take the governor's share, just "that the account would become known," Monk said.

Ultimately, Monk said he saw not a cent of the money.

"Do you know what happened to it?" Niewoehner asked.

"No," he said.

Niewoehner fast-forwarded to 2007 or 2008, to a conversation during which Monk said he and Blagojevich were alone in the governor's office. They discussed an FBI investigation.

Blagojevich told Monk not to ever talk about the "1, 2, 3, 4" reference.

On the witness stand, Monk mimicked Blagojevich's gestures, putting up his fingers one at a time, then running a single finger across his throat. In the courtroom, Blagojevich grew unsettled in his chair. He leaned forward and stared right at Monk. As Monk gestured, Blagojevich sat back hard in his chair and muttered something inaudible. Monk's allegations contradicted the image Blagojevich had attempted to paint of himself—and of his case— over the preceding year. This wasn't just political talk caught on tape. Monk's testimony put the former governor into new territory: that of a dirty politician looking to line his pockets from the very onset of his administration.

Monk went on at length about how state appointments were given out under Blagojevich's reign. Monk said Rezko believed "some of these board spots were high profile enough and prestigious enough...that at a minimum some of these people ought to be donating $25,000," Monk said. These were positions like trusteeships at the University of Illinois, the State Board of Investment, and the like, Monk said.

Blagojevich called these positions his "ambassadorships," Monk said, referring to the notion that ambassadorships are appointed by presidents as thank-yous for big campaign contributions.

As the testimony wore on, Monk revealed something highly charged that threatened to put Blagojevich in a negative light. Monk said he had accepted envelopes stuffed with tens of thousands of dollars in cash from Rezko starting in the spring of 2004. The cash came in overnight envelopes, usually $10,000 at a time. Monk accepted the cash seven or nine times, he said, including once as a gift at his wedding. Rezko also brought in contractors to finish Monk's basement at his Park Ridge home in the fall of 2005. Monk was already doing pretty much everything Rezko asked, he said, and Rezko didn't ask for anything in particular in exchange for the payments. Monk never told Blagojevich about the money and said he never witnessed Blagojevich similarly taking cash from Rezko.

Monk left Blagojevich's employ in 2006. He went on to work as a state lobbyist, and his salary went up exponentially. In 2007, he made $750,000. In 2008, "about a million." Monk detailed the gubernatorial campaign, saying Blagojevich handily beat his opponents in fundraising.

Blagojevich's strategy had been to "outwork" Judy Baar Topinka in the 2006 election, Monk said. He outspent and outraised Topinka in the campaign, Monk said. Monk described Blagojevich as a man so consumed by raising money, and thus power, for himself that he was willing to trade a Senate seat appointment to kill an ethics bill.

Monk testified that a call from Barack Obama in 2008 unwittingly derailed a deal hatched by Blagojevich and then-Illinois Senate President Emil Jones. Monk testified that Blagojevich told him that Jones (who has since retired) would not call an ethics bill that Blagojevich strongly opposed if "Rod named him to Obama's Senate seat if Obama won in November."

"Did you understand he was serious?" Niewoehner asked.

"Yes," Monk said.

Obama himself then phoned Jones and told him to call the bill for a vote, Monk said. Jones told Blagojevich he was going back on the deal.

Monk said Blagojevich pushed to raise more money in 2008 but ran into brick walls. The next gubernatorial election wasn't for another two years.

"A lot of people we were asking for money didn't see a need to be donating money," Monk said. Plus, there was a presidential election. "We had Barack Obama in Chicago running for president," and they were hitting up some of the same people for both campaigns, Monk said. And there was one more reason: "The economy was not good and there were federal investigations that I'm sure was [sic] concerning donors," Monk said.

The prosecution began playing tapes that largely focused on the shakedown of Maywood Park racetrack owner Johnny Johnston, who was Monk's client in 2008. They played one call between the Blagojevich brothers, during which Rob cracked a rare smile, as did the usually straight-faced court reporter. "I tell you what, very impressed, very delightful wife," Rob tells Rod on the call. "She loves our hair by the way. She loves your hair, loves my hair, because it's all real."

A December 3, 2008, recording from a campaign office bug captured Blagojevich and Monk talking in person at the Friends of Blagojevich office about the Johnston contribution. Prosecutors contended that on this call, Monk and Blagojevich rehearsed the shakedown. By this point, both houses of the legislature had passed racetrack legislation of concern to Johnston; it only awaited the governor's signature to become law. Every day the bill went unsigned, Monk said, his client lost $9,000 in subsidies. Still, Monk said on the recordings he would push Johnston to hand over the check.

"Give us the money. One has nothing to do with the other," Monk said he would tell Johnston, referring to the contribution and the legislation. "Give us the fucking money." Monk eventually approached Johnston with the conversation. He wasn't as forceful as he and Blagojevich had planned. But the message got across, he said.

"I wanted to let him know why the bill wasn't getting signed," Monk testified—namely, because the governor wanted $100,000 to sign it—"and as a result, he should give the contribution now."

Adam livened up the room when he began his animated cross-examination of Monk. Adam's questions cut deep into the history of Monk and Blagojevich's friendship, which began when they met at Pepperdine Law School in California. Adam said that Monk and Blagojevich lived together in law school, they shared secrets, talked about girls. Monk agreed.

"Rod trusted you," Adam said. "Is there anything from your relationship in Pepperdine that would cause you to believe you'd be here?" he continued dramatically, pointing to the witness chair. Then, pointing to the defense table, he added, "And he'd be there?"

"You're his best friend, aren't you?" Adam asked. Monk agreed: "Yeah, good friend."

Adam vigorously attacked Monk's credibility as a witness, arguing that what he told jurors was the prosecutors' version of the truth in exchange for a sentence one-tenth as long as the one he might have faced. He grew animated as he asked Monk if he remembered any details from the meetings where the four agreed to split up money from state deals.

"I don't remember," Monk said repeatedly. Adam neared him, then paced away. He pointed to the ex-governor and pointed in the air. It was the first time in Monk's adult life that he was to commit a felony, and he couldn't recall "one!" detail about what Rezko wrote on that board? Blagojevich was sitting sideways with one arm lazily lying on the courtroom table, looking as if he was enjoying the show.

"I don't know if we gave that much thought where the money was going to go," Monk said. Blagojevich quietly laughed to himself, then put his hand over his mouth to suppress his smile.

On June 15, 2010, prosecutors called Joseph Aramanda to the stand. Aramanda, a friend and former business associate of Rezko's, was significant as a means for the prosecution to bolster Monk's testimony about Blagojevich agreeing to split up cash.

Aramanda, who testified under a letter of immunity, said Rezko had told him that Blagojevich, while governor, had been involved in a deal with Rezko where fees would be split between himself and his "inner circle." Rezko had proposed that Aramanda act as an intermediary with the Teachers' Retirement System and receive fees from TRS investments with different firms, according to court records. Aramanda testified that Rezko invited him to be part of that business venture. His annual yearly salary would be $250,000. Aramanda said he thought that was shockingly low, given that the transactions could rake in $1 million or more per deal and there would likely be multiple deals each year.

Aramanda asked Rezko what was going to happen to the rest of the money. The answer was that it would be split among other partners. Aramanda backed up Monk's claim—that sharing in the proceeds from that proposed deal would be Blagojevich, Monk, and Kelly.

"I was uncomfortable with the situation," Aramanda said of the proposed venture. "I thought it was wrong." Aramanda said he refused to take part in it.

On cross-examination, Michael Gillespie, one of Blagojevich's attorneys, took great pains to make sure Aramanda explained who else was at Rezko's mansion the day he met Blagojevich: specifically, Barack Obama. Aramanda said the event was a fundraiser for both Obama and Blagojevich. Aramanda testified that Rezko asked him to write a $10,000 campaign contribution check to Obama.

"Isn't it true that Mr. Rezko asked you to make a check for $10,000 out to Friends of Obama?" Gillespie asked. Aramanda acknowledged that he gave $10,000 in campaign cash to Obama's Senate campaign on March 5, 2004, according to records. In Rezko's criminal trial, prosecutors said that Aramanda had received an illegal $250,000 "finder's fee" tied to a state teacher-pension investment deal. Prosecutors also said that Aramanda did no work for the money, and that some of it was used to pay a Rezko debt. According to prosecutors, it was a portion of that $250,000 that was routed back to Obama's campaign when he was running for U.S. Senate.

Aramanda said Rezko asked him to make the donation for him; it is a violation of campaign finance laws to make straw donations. Obama—who has said he had no idea at the time that the

Aramanda contribution was tainted in any way—later gave the Aramanda money to charity, as well as tens of thousands of dollars more from Rezko.

The next substantive witness, called on June 16, 2010, was Ali Ata—the man who crafted a last-minute deal with the feds in 2008 to help sink Rezko. Ata had pleaded guilty that year in one courtroom, then almost immediately walked across the courthouse and took the witness stand in the Rezko trial. He gave some jaw-dropping information to the government, including that he delivered black plastic bags stuffed with cash to Rezko to pay contractors threatening to slap an embarrassing lien on the governor's home. Ata said he got more than $100,000 in cash out of a safe at Rezko's request and that he and Rezko drove to Kelly's home and delivered $50,000 of the money.

That didn't come up at the Blagojevich trial, though. Ata, who was director of the Illinois Finance Authority under Blagojevich, detailed how he pulled off an income-tax scam regarding a commercial property he sold with Rezko at the intersection of Addison and Kimball streets in Chicago. He also began to discuss his relationship with Blagojevich, saying he started raising money for Blagojevich's gubernatorial race in 2002. "Mr. Blagojevich called and asked for my support," Ata said. "I held two fundraisers and contributed money on my own." Ata testified he went to Rezko's real estate office on August 30, 2002—shortly before Blagojevich was elected governor in November 2002—to drop off a $25,000 campaign contribution to Blagojevich. Rezko brought Ata back to a conference room where Ata met with Rezko, Kelly, Monk, and state Rep. Jay Hoffman, a Democrat from the Downstate city of Collinsville. At that point, Rezko told the group how Ata had been a "team player" and should be considered for a position within Blagojevich's future administration.

Then, in July 2003, Rezko raised the possibility of Ata becoming director of the Illinois Finance Authority, a new agency. Rezko asked Ata for a $50,000 contribution.

"I told him I can do 25," meaning $25,000, Ata testified. He made that second contribution at a Navy Pier fundraiser for Blagojevich that same month. At the fundraiser, Ata said he had a conversation with Blagojevich in which Blagojevich thanked him for his support. Blagojevich also said he was aware Ata was up for a job in Blagojevich's administration.

"It better be a job where you'd make some money," Ata said Blagojevich told him.

Ata said he found the statement strange but didn't react to it at the time. Eventually, he got the Illinois Finance Authority post in January 2004. Ata repeated a charge he first leveled in 2008—that Rezko had told him that President George W. Bush's top adviser, Karl Rove, was working to replace Patrick Fitzgerald as U.S. Attorney in the Northern District of Illinois. Rove had repeatedly denied that charge, but Ata believed Rezko. Ata said the possibility that Fitzgerald might be replaced contributed to his willingness to lie to the FBI in 2005. In the end, of course, Fitzgerald was not replaced.

The prosecution next called its first "victim" to the stand: Johnny Johnston. Johnston began by testifying about a December 3, 2008, meeting that happened right after Monk's meeting with Blagojevich, at which Monk said they discussed shaking down Johnston. For his part, Johnston said he purposely planted his father—"an ornery S.O.B."—in his meeting with Monk so Monk wouldn't bring up the subject of the contribution he and Blagojevich wanted. It didn't work—Monk brought it up anyway, in the vestibule on his way out, Johnston testified. Monk said he had spoken to the governor, who was concerned that if he signed the racetrack bill, Johnston would not make a contribution.

"I said, 'I thought that's what the governor might be thinking. Your suggestion of a contribution at this time is inappropriate,'" Johnston testified. "[Monk] turned to me and kind of rubbed his hands together and said, 'OK, different subject matter. I really need you to get a contribution in by the end of the year,'" Johnston testified. Johnston again tried to dodge the subject, he said, but he felt pressured to give money and was uncomfortable.

Next up that day was Bradley Tusk, a one-time deputy governor in the Blagojevich administration, who testified about another alleged shakedown scheme involving Blagojevich. Tusk said that while he was deputy governor, Blagojevich told him he wanted a message delivered to then-U.S. Rep. Rahm Emanuel: a $2-million grant for the Chicago Academy, a school in Emanuel's district, was on hold unless his brother, well-known Hollywood agent Ari Emanuel, would hold a fundraiser.

Tusk said he didn't deliver the message but called Blagojevich's lawyer to tell him, "You need to get your client under control." Almost as an aside, the prosecution had Tusk talk about what it was like working for Blagojevich. Tusk said that just finding him on some days was tricky. He mentioned hunting down Blagojevich at his tailor to sign pending legislation. Tusk was often tasked with signing or vetoing bills himself.

On that same day John Harris took the stand. The former chief of staff testified that it wasn't a state of Illinois representative who offered him a chief of staff position—but Kelly, who at the time was just a fundraiser for Blagojevich. Harris said he met with Kelly for coffee, and Kelly offered him the job.

"They had a team not too familiar with government...not much government or administration experience," Harris said. "They thought I would be a valuable asset and addition to the team."

In the fall of 2006, Harris said, he started getting phone calls from both Tusk and Emanuel's office about a school grant that was turning out to be a big headache. Emanuel wanted to know where the money was; Tusk told Harris that the governor would not approve the release of funds. So, Harris testified, he spoke to the governor. "He seemed to be familiar with it and told me not to approve the release of funds, that he had not approved the release of funds," Harris said. The prosecution's charges alleged that Blagojevich was withholding those payments in an effort to strong-arm Emanuel.

By way of background, Harris said Blagojevich had instructed him to cut off particular people in the past. He said Blagojevich told him to block two firms, including Citibank, from getting state business, as retaliation for not giving his wife Patti a job.

Patti had just gotten her Series 7 securities license, and Blagojevich was anxious to find her work, Harris testified. He said Blagojevich asked Harris to meet with some business contacts on her behalf. Harris did, reaching out to two acquaintances, including one at Citibank, he said. But the networking attempts failed, and the governor was not pleased, he testified. "He told me to make sure Citibank doesn't get any more state work, and to make sure that John Rogers doesn't get any more state work," Harris testified. "He didn't feel they had done enough to help Patti." Harris told an "agitated" and "angry" Blagojevich that cutting the firms off would be impossible, that he didn't have control over their bond work. When Harris later learned Citibank was in line to win a major state deal, he said he purposely kept Blagojevich in the dark. He testified that "I knew he would be upset."

Harris covered substantial ground in little time. He supported Monk's testimony that there was a deal between Blagojevich and Emil Jones to kill ethics legislation in exchange for Jones replacing Obama in the Senate. Harris said that during an October 6, 2008, conversation in a car, Blagojevich brought up the Senate seat for the first time since the Jones debacle.

"So what do you think I can get for the Senate seat?" Harris said the governor asked.

"What do you mean? For you?" Harris asked. "You can get a new ally or reward an ally, that's what you can get."

Blagojevich then looked away and was quiet, Harris testified. But that wasn't the last of it, he added, describing two more conversations with the governor about what he could get for the appointment. At one point, the conversation turned to cash. Blagojevich wondered how much he could get for the seat from several interested parties, including Blair Hull, who had been defeated by Obama in the 2004 Democratic primary for U.S. senator. "I told him, 'You can't get money for the Senate seat. You shouldn't even consider that as an option.' And we moved on," Harris testified.

Then, later that same month, Blagojevich, Harris, and the governor's attorney, Bill Quinlan, were again discussing Senate seat possibilities. Blagojevich brought up how he might profit from the appointment, perhaps by putting "money into a 501(c)(3)." Harris said Quinlan became stern with Blagojevich.

"You can't ever joke like that. You can't talk like that," Harris said Quinlan told him. "You know, whether you're serious or not, don't say things like that."

Chapter Eleven

Playing the Tapes

It was two days before a historic election, Harris testified, when Obama's people called Harris. Harris was shopping with his kids at a Payless shoe store on November 2, 2008, when he got a call from Rahm Emanuel, who told Harris that Obama was interested in seeing a "close friend" of his appointed to his seat. Harris said he understood that friend to be Valerie Jarrett.

"[Emanuel] asked whether it would be helpful if Senator Obama called the governor to advocate for this individual," Harris testified of the phone call. "I said sure." The next day he spoke to Blagojevich about Emanuel conveying Barack Obama's interest in having Valerie Jarrett appointed to the Senate seat.

"Should I have Barack call Rod?" Harris said Rahm asked him. Harris said it would help, and he's heard laughing on tape as he relays this conversation to Blagojevich. "You may get a call from him or Dave," he goes on.

"Dave who?" Blagojevich says.

"Axelrod," Harris says. Harris is heard on tape explaining that he believes Obama is serious. "[Obama] wouldn't leave it to osmosis or the media. He very much cares about this. It's his definite desire for Valerie."

Blagojevich says, "We should get something for that. Could I? What about Health and Human Services, can I get that?" Harris testified that this was a reference to a cabinet appointment. "What could I honestly think I might get a shot at getting?" Blagojevich asks.

"Well, besides good things for Illinois, good things for Illinois?" Harris says. In court, Harris said what's made clear in that conversation: "that [Blagojevich] was seeking something for himself as well."

Back on the tape, Blagojevich wonders what else might be available to him: "I mean, what other cabinet position would be not stupid?" he is heard asking. "UN ambassador?"

"Yeah, I don't think that's realistic or serious," Harris replies.

"Shit, that would be cool, huh?" Blagojevich says, laughing.

On the call, Blagojevich also explores appointing himself, describing it as the "ace in the hole." Then he brings up the Health and Human Service appointment by Obama. Harris urges Blagojevich not to shoot too high to start. Instead, he suggests, let the Obama camp make the first move.

"Let them feel like they're helping you," Harris says. "Let them come to you first."

"Let's go down the pecking order. What else is good?" Blagojevich asks. Harris says he thinks Obama would "do an ambassadorship."

Blagojevich replied, "OK. I'm interested. How about India? South Africa?…That's realistic?"

Harris explained his reasoning from the stand, saying, "An ambassadorship in some small country somewhere would pretty much sideline [Blagojevich] for the rest of his political life" and therefore might have been appealing to Obama.

On the tape, Blagojevich is clearly taken with the India idea.

"I'm the governor of a $58-billion corporation, why can't I be ambassador to India?" he asks.

"Canada? France?" Blagojevich goes on, floating ideas for other countries to which he might be appointed ambassador.

"All those are easier than India," Harris replies. But Blagojevich might face an uphill battle. "It's the Rezko issue," Harris is heard saying. "I think your qualifications are there. It's not about your qualifications."

Blagojevich later called Patti to float the idea of moving to India. They are heard discussing what she would feed her daughters and how congested the running paths would likely be in India.

Harris and Blagojevich are also heard discussing other alternatives for the seat—including Bill Daley, the former U.S. commerce secretary and brother of Mayor Richard Daley, and Lisa Madigan. However, Harris testified, those were basically decoys, not serious alternatives. Harris and Blagojevich at one point discuss leaking a potential Lisa Madigan appointment to *Sun-Times* columnist Michael Sneed.

Harris explained from the stand, "Michael Sneed is a woman who writes a political gossip column for a local paper—a page that a lot of politicians read before the sports." Hamilton asked, then, if Harris and Blagojevich were talking about leaking "false information" to Sneed.

"Yes," Harris replied.

Blagojevich's alleged attempt to clear out the editorial board at the *Chicago Tribune* was the next topic to come up, as prosecutors played a recorded call during which Blagojevich was heard telling Harris that the critical pieces on the *Tribune*'s editorial page had better stop.

"I understood him to say…let them know that we would not be going forward with involvement with the sale of Cubs and Wrigley Field and we would not be providing our assistance if they continued to beat up the governor on its editorial page," Harris testified.

Hamilton asked Harris what message Blagojevich wanted sent to the *Tribune*.

"Stop or else," Harris said. "Stop with the bad editorials, or else we won't go forward with this."

"What is it that he wanted?" Hamilton asked Harris about Blagojevich. "A new editorial board," Harris replied.

Throughout Harris's testimony, jurors also heard how Blagojevich spent his days as governor. He passed much of his time at his home, ordering two state-paid workers to research future high-paying jobs for him. The secret recordings revealed that the plotting was constant. In one call, Blagojevich can be heard snapping at Patti on the phone as she's looking up salary information for him.

"You're just wasting fucking time. We're making it up. We're saying this is what I want...this is the deal."

Later on the tape, Blagojevich and Harris discuss a call Harris got from John Wyma relaying a message from the Obama camp. This was significant because it showed that Wyma, a Blagojevich friend and lobbyist, had contact with both the Obama camp and Blagojevich at the same time he had been cooperating with federal officials.

"Rahm asked [Wyma] to deliver the message—the president-elect would be very pleased if you appointed Valerie and he would be, uh, thankful and appreciative" for a Valerie Jarrett appointment, Harris tells Blagojevich on the recorded call.

"They're not willing to give me anything but appreciation—fuck them," Blagojevich says. In the background, a children's TV show is heard playing, and a child is heard talking.

As the trial kept up its quick pace, each recording seemed to trump the next.

In one tape, Rob Blagojevich attempts to dispense a dose of sanity to his younger brother.

Rod suggests that he should appoint to the Senate his deputy governor, Louanner Peters, because she could then step aside before he would get impeached, leaving Rod himself to assume the Senate seat.

"Oh Jesus!" Rob can be heard saying.

"What's better," Blagojevich replies, "that or being impeached?"

"Neither one! Neither one! It's so transparent. What is the public going to think?...I don't like that option at all," Rob says forcefully.

In another tape, Blagojevich is heard floating yet another idea—asking the president-elect to ask Warren Buffett or Bill Gates to throw $15 million into a healthcare-related charity account that Blagojevich could manage and live off. In exchange, of course, he'd appoint Jarrett to Obama's Senate seat.

As it turned out, Valerie Jarrett eventually publically removed herself from consideration for the Senate appointment. At that point, Emanuel called Harris with a list of "acceptable" names, saying it was from Obama, according to Harris. They were: rising Democratic star and disabled Iraq War veteran Tammy Duckworth; Illinois State Comptroller Dan Hynes; Jesse Jackson Jr.; and U.S. Rep. Jan Schakowsky.

Blagojevich called it a "B.S. list." Lending credence to Blagojevich's characterization was the fact that union representatives Tom Balanoff and Andy Stern—Obama's intermediaries—had previously told Blagojevich that Jesse Jackson Jr. should not be a considered for the appointment.

Emanuel's call to Harris about Obama's "acceptable" list of potential appointees came just days after he made a phone call to Wyma sending a message from the president about Jarrett. Wyma had been cooperating with federal investigators for weeks at the time of the phone call. Emanuel told Harris that no one else from the Obama camp was allowed to talk about the Senate seat besides him, Harris said.

Blagojevich was now heard on tape saying that the next senator must satisfy three criteria, "legal, personal, and political," in relation to himself.

In another set of recordings played for jurors, Blagojevich and Harris float names for the Senate seat. It is apparent from Blagojevich's breathlessness and the clanking of weights that the former governor is working out at home while he is on the call. The person Blagojevich is heard suggesting for the Senate seat on this call: Oprah Winfrey.

"That's crazy," Harris says.

"That's where you're wrong," Blagojevich replies. "She made Obama...She's a Democrat."

Harris responds, "You're looking for a celebrity to be your friend?"

"She's so up there, so high..." Blagojevich says.

Blagojevich continues brainstorming. "Maybe a black Albert Einstein," he suggests. Hearing that, one African-American juror gently shook her head.

On the recording, Blagojevich is insistent that they "bolster the list" of potential appointees, even if it means looking outside of Illinois.

"Who outside of Illinois might fit the bill?" he is heard asking Harris. He mentions Arnold Schwarzenegger as an example. Harris tries to talk him out of it.

"Picking somebody outside of Illinois has a whole host of problems," Harris tells him. "[They'll say], 'There are 13 million residents [in Illinois], Rod hates them all.'"

A later tape captured Blagojevich talking of appointing Jesse Jackson Jr., whom he refers to as "über-African American." At that, an African-American juror laughed quietly and had to put a hand over her mouth. A juror beside her flashed a knowing smile. This was a rare show of expression from the usually poker-faced jurors.

Under cross-examination by Sam Adam Sr., Harris acknowledged he heard Blagojevich talk of a deal where Lisa Madigan would get the seat in exchange for having her powerful father pass a Blagojevich legislative bill that would include healthcare expansion.

"I heard him say that," Harris said.

"You understood the passion of the governor was for healthcare, didn't you?" Adam asked.

"I understood he was passionate about that, yes."

Thomas Balanoff said he was at dinner the night before the November 4, 2008, presidential election when he got a call from a blocked number. He hit "ignore" on his phone and continued with his meal.

Later, he dialed up to hear his messages: "I walked outside, listened to it, and it was from President Obama," Balanoff said.

"Tom, this is Barack, give me a call," Obama said on the message.

After Balanoff sent word through an Obama aide to call him back, Obama returned his call later that night. Balanoff was pumping gas.

"Tom, I want to talk to you with regard to the Senate seat," Obama told him. Balanoff said Obama told him he had two criteria: someone who was good for the citizens of Illinois and who could be elected in 2010. Obama said he wasn't publicly coming out in support of anyone, but he believed Valerie Jarrett would fit the bill. "I would much prefer she [work in the White House], but she does want to be senator and she does meet those two criteria," Balanoff said Obama told him. "I said, 'Thank you, I'm going to reach out to Governor Blagojevich.'"

The morning of the election, Balanoff said he had a phone discussion with Jarrett in which he talked about her wanting the Senate seat.

"Didn't Barack call you last night?" Jarrett asked, according to Balanoff. "Well, I am interested," he said she told him.

Balanoff then described a November 6, 2008, meeting he had with Blagojevich to recommend Jarrett for the seat. Blagojevich responded that he was in "active discussions" with the Madigans about appointing Lisa Madigan and was holding out for a legislative package with the House speaker. Balanoff believed he was bluffing.

"I said that could be months. He said, "Yeah.' I said, Valerie Jarrett, I don't believe she has that kind of time," Balanoff testified. Blagojevich then turned the conversation to a cabinet position, Balanoff said. "He said, 'You know, I love being governor, but my real passion is healthcare,'" and then he asked about the Health and Human Services cabinet post.

"I told him that's not going to happen," Balanoff testified. "He said, 'Is that because of all the investigations around me?'"

Balanoff then testified that after the election, he met with both Jarrett and Illinois State Treasurer Alexi Giannoulias about Jarrett's possible appointment to the Senate. Balanoff said he asked Giannoulias to set up the meeting. The three met at the Aon Center in downtown Chicago on November 7. Balanoff said he told Jarrett about his meeting the day before with Blagojevich.

"I said, 'He said some goofy stuff...[that] he could be secretary of Health and Human Services.'" Balanoff testified. "I told her I told him that wasn't going to happen. We both laughed."

Balanoff said he planned to tell Blagojevich that if he didn't appoint Jarrett, the governor couldn't expect future help from the SEIU, a major Democratic contributor.

"I was going to use our union's influence to make a good decision," Balanoff said. Balanoff said he tried meeting with Blagojevich that Saturday to have coffee, but Blagojevich told him he'd be out of town.

"I really felt that he blew me off," Balanoff testified. He then called Jarrett, he said.

"I'm really sorry, I thought you'd be a really good senator for the state of Illinois," Balanoff said he told Jarrett on the phone call. In the courtroom, Blagojevich adjusted his watch, pursed his lips, and shifted considerably in his chair during Balanoff's testimony.

Balanoff said that on November 12, 2008, after Blagojevich heard Jarrett might go to the White House, the then-governor called him. Blagojevich said he wanted a 501(c)(4) foundation set up and in exchange he'd appoint Jarrett.

"Somehow if I could get this foundation set up he would be open to appointing Valerie Jarrett," Balanoff said. He further explained that Blagojevich wanted to head it up himself. He hoped "[t]hat when he was no longer governor he could run this 501(c)(4)," Balanoff said, explaining another taped telephone call. On the tape Blagojevich tells Balanoff that millionaires George Soros or Warren Buffett "could put $15 million, $20 million overnight. And then we can help our new senator, Valerie Jarrett, go out and push that."

How did Balanoff understand that conversation?, he was asked by the prosecution. "That in fact he was making this proposal and in return Valerie Jarrett would be appointed," he testified. On the recording, Balanoff was heard saying he would run the proposal "up the flagpole."

"Who was the flagpole?" prosecutor Reid Schar asked. Balanoff replied, "I was," adding that he was just trying to get off the phone. "I never had any intention of taking this anywhere." However, Balanoff did immediately call Jarrett and leave her a message saying, "Call me. I have a quick question for you."

Schar asked, "Did you ever hear back from her?"

Balanoff replied, "No, I did not."

Balanoff said he brought up to Blagojevich the possibility of appointing U.S. Rep. Jan Schakowsky.

Nope, said Blagojevich. "If she had any ancestors who came over on slave ships she'd be fine," he elaborated from the witness chair.

Sorosky cross-examined Balanoff and focused on the question of whether Blagojevich explicitly said he'd appoint Jarrett in exchange for a cabinet appointment.

"Yes or no?" Sorosky persisted.

"No," Balanoff said. Sorosky needled Balanoff over his conversations with Blagojevich. He asked Balanoff whether he ever flagged any issues with Blagojevich's requests for a cabinet position or a 501(c)(4) foundation as Jarrett sought the Senate seat.

"You never tell the governor he's doing anything wrong?" Sorosky asked.

"That's correct," replied Balanoff.

"You tell him you're going to accommodate him?...You don't tell him: 'Hey you're stepping out of bounds, you're going too far, or I think that's improper,' do you?" Sorosky asked.

Balanoff answered, "No, I do not."

Next to the witness stand, on June 29, 2010, was Doug Scofield, former chief of staff for U.S. Rep. Luis Gutierrez, who had dropped his job in Washington to take on a deputy governor job during Blagojevich's first term as governor. He said he left Blagojevich after three months.

"I was uncomfortable with some of the professional aspects for me," Scofield said. "I was particularly concerned about Tony Rezko and Chris Kelly—two individuals who were involved in the campaign. I found that once we were elected...the two were significantly involved. Certainly in suggesting candidates for state jobs."

Scofield, though, came right back to work for Blagojevich. In 2005, he took a role in communications with Blagojevich's campaign. In 2008, Scofield said he had a conversation with Blagojevich about the possibility that Obama would win the presidency. Blagojevich wasn't happy.

"I think he was frustrated by it," Scofield said. "He was a fellow Illinois politician and seemed to be on the verge of national success. It was clear to me there was some jealousy...as to what Senator Obama was doing."

Since the day of his arrest, the most infamous quote associated with Rod Blagojevich was the phrase he used to describe the Senate appointment with Scofield on November 5, 2008: "It's fucking golden." During Scofield's testimony, jurors heard Blagojevich speak those words on a recorded conversation.

"UN ambassador, I'd take that," Blagojevich was also heard saying on the call.

"'You Russian motherfuckers.' Can you see me? [Laughs] All right, anyway, um, but those are not reachable. But, you know. [Sighs] I told my nephew Alex, he just turned 26 today. I said: 'Alex,' you know, I call him for his birthday, and I says, 'It's just too bad you're not four years older 'cause I could a given you a U.S. Senate seat for your birthday.'"

"Yeah," Scofield is heard saying.

Blagojevich adds, "You know what I mean?"

Scofield laughs and repeats, "Yeah."

"I mean I, I've got this thing and it's fucking golden," Blagojevich continues.

"Right," Scofield interjects.

"And I, I'm just not giving it up for fucking nothing."

In court, Schar asked Scofield, "What do you understand him to want?"

"He wants an appointment from the president," Scofield answered. Scofield testified that the cabinet position was discussed by

Balanoff and Jarrett, and that he himself had discussed the prospect with union member Jerry Morrison, who was skeptical.

"The president-elect and the people around the president-elect wanted to get away from Chicago politics," Scofield testified.

That testimony by Scofield set up the playing of a call where Blagojevich was heard equating Chicago politics with Rezko, whose relationship with Obama had been an issue in the presidential campaign.

"She's holding hers with two hands...sort of clinging to it. Me, I've got the whole thing wrapped around my arms," Blagojevich is heard saying about Jarrett and the Senate seat. The courtroom grew quiet during this portion of the recording.

On the next recording played, Blagojevich is on a conference call with his advisers, including political strategist Doug Sosnik, and they're telling him to appoint Valerie Jarrett for nothing.

"They all leave town and I'm stuck with gridlock...impeachment...and a fucking president who's all talk and no give?" Blagojevich is heard saying. "That's what you're recommending to me, Doug?"

Replies Sosnik, "Yes."

Blagojevich is heard saying he talked to "the Jacksons" over the weekend and wants Scofield to tell Balanoff that Jesse Jackson Jr. is a prospect again.

"I over-promised on Jesse Jr....He's in the mix all of a sudden, OK?" Blagojevich says, giggling. "Joe Stroud [a wealthy state donor] was part of it. I'll tell you when I see you," he says. "I'm not ruling him out."

In another call, Wyma again comes up.

"Should I just have Wyma do it?" Blagojevich says on the recording, referring to the fact that he wanted Wyma to deliver a message to Emanuel about Blagojevich's foundation idea. Blagojevich is heard asking Harris that Wyma be used to take a message to the Obama camp.

"Can you call Wyma? Have him call Rahm. I want a 501(c)(4)," Blagojevich says. Harris replies that Scofield should do it.

"So the mission for Wyma is essentially to put it in Rahm's head that we need him to help to fund it," Blagojevich says on the recording.

Scofield and Blagojevich didn't know it, but at that point Wyma had been cooperating with FBI agents for weeks. He had been asked to wear a wire, but had refused. Wyma's cooperation served as the probable cause basis for the feds to set up its wiretaps. Scofield testified that he called Wyma to deliver the message that Blagojevich wanted a foundation set up for him in exchange for appointing Jarrett to the Senate seat.

"I said 'John, every now and then we get asked to do something that is ridiculous even by our standards,'" Scofield testified. "But I've been asked to pass this along, so I'm passing this along."

Blagojevich's defense lawyers objected twice to Scofield's remark about the request being "ridiculous."

"If the goal of your objection was to stop his answer, you've succeeded," Judge Zagel said.

Scofield continued, "I said, Rod is really around the bend on this Senate stuff, so here's what he said to me and I'll pass it on to you."

Schar asked, "Did Mr. Wyma express any concerns about the message?"

"He seemed slightly confused about it," Scofield said. "He wanted to clarify that it was related to the Senate seat...which I had said within the first five seconds of picking up the phone."

Scofield continued, "We talked about this idea of funders [for the foundation Blagojevich wanted], which we both found a little implausible." Scofield then said he was under the impression that Wyma would not pass the idea along to Emanuel. He didn't hear from Wyma again.

Defense lawyer Aaron Goldstein, cross-examining, pointed out that Scofield is heard saying on a recording that "the only one [deal] worth doing because they give something is Valerie."

"Your words?" Goldstein asked. Scofield agreed that they were.

Goldstein was trying to show that Scofield continued to talk to Blagojevich about the Senate seat during multiple calls. Goldstein asked if Scofield was encouraging Blagojevich's efforts to get something in exchange for the Senate seat.

"He may have certainly taken it as encouragement. I certainly didn't mean it as encouragement," Scofield said. He said that while it appeared he was agreeing with Blagojevich's efforts on the recordings, he didn't mean what he was saying.

Goldstein asked, "I guess what you're saying is that you're lying to the governor?"

Scofield replied, "I was telling him what I thought he wanted to hear."

Scofield was not charged with wrongdoing.

In November 2008, while Rod Blagojevich was plotting and scheming with his advisers, he was also recorded complaining loudly that he was desperate for cash.

"Amy is going to college in six years, and we can't afford it," Blagojevich screamed on a November 10 call. "I feel like I'm fucking my children."

Four days later, he dropped $429 on two ties at Saks Fifth Avenue. Two days after that, he hit Saks again and spent another $429 on another pair of neckties. A few weeks later, it was time for a custom suit. That price tag: $4,000.

According to credit card records introduced to the jury, this spree was just a small part of the more than $400,000 Blagojevich spent on fine clothing, ties, footwear, and even underwear in his tenure as governor. It was discovered that the Blagojeviches spent more on fine clothing than on their mortgage, childcare, travel, or private school expenses in the years that Blagojevich served as governor, according to trial testimony. Many of these expenditures came as the family was swimming in debt. The receipts showed that Blagojevich dropped hundreds of dollars at a time on ties at Saks Fifth Avenue and thousands of dollars on custom Oxxford suits and pricey Allen Edmonds footwear. In a matter of days in 2006, Blagojevich spent $5,000 on an Oxxford suit, $1,400 on Geneva custom shirts, $63 on Hanro underwear, and $214 on ties. IRS agent Shari Schindler testified that she totaled up all the various expenditures from 2002 to 2008 and that, of the top 15 businesses or people receiving money from Blagojevich, four were clothing related. That included more than $205,000 in spending at Tom James Clothing/Oxxford, a custom suit maker. After the family's mortgage company, this was the second-biggest recipient of money on the list.

Perhaps anticipating that his spending habits would be on full display, Blagojevich often repeated the ties he wore during his trial. In the courtroom, everyone appeared to be checking out Blago-jevich's ties—it was light blue with a dark design on July 1, 2010. On his way out of court that day, Rod Blagojevich's brother, Rob, stopped and smiled.

"For the record, I buy my ties on sale," he said.

When it came to the Blagojevich family's income, there was tes-timony that same day that Patti made money from Rezko's com-pany, Rezmar, for doing nothing.

Testifying under a grant of immunity, Robert Williams, for-mer chief financial officer of Rezmar, said Patti was paid $12,000 a month for what was recorded in Rezmar books as "consulting."

Carrie Hamilton asked if Williams was aware of any consulting work Patti Blagojevich did.

"I was not," he said.

Jurors also heard Blagojevich in yet another expletive-laden conference call reacting to his advisers telling him again that he shouldn't expect anything from Obama in exchange for appointing his favored candidate to the Senate.

"You guys are telling me...give this motherfucker his senator. Fuck him! For nothing? Fuck him!" an angry Blagojevich was heard snarling.

The advisers also told him that if he tried to appoint himself senator, he would be "a national joke."

"We're stuck....This world is passing me by, and I'm stuck in this job as governor," Blagojevich moans. "I'm stuck."

The prosecution had to lay the groundwork for the most damning allegation: that Blagojevich was scheming to take a $1.5-million campaign contribution from a Jesse Jackson Jr. supporter in exchange for appointing Jackson. To do that, the government called Rajinder Bedi—the same fundraiser Blagojevich once referred to as "my Sikh warrior."

According to prosecutors, Bedi, Jackson, and Nayak all met at the 312 Chicago restaurant on October 28, 2008. The conversation turned to Jackson's interest in the Senate seat, which would be up for grabs once Obama became president in a matter of days.

"The thing that's significant: Nayak says, 'I will raise $1 million for Blagojevich if he appoints you [Jackson] to the Senate seat,'" Niewoehner told Judge James Zagel with the jury out of the room. Niewoehner said Bedi heard Nayak tell Jackson this. He did not offer any more details.

Hours later, he said, Bedi met with Rob Blagojevich.

"That statement...leads Bedi to mention [to Rob Blagojevich] that Nayak is interested in doing fundraising for Blagojevich, and he wants Jackson appointed," Niewoehner said. Prosecutors were able to reveal very few details of the October 28 meeting, which was largely discussed with jurors out of the room. Ultimately, Zagel severely limited what Bedi could testify about.

In cross-examination, though, Bedi admitted to Michael Ettinger that Rob Blagojevich told him flat out that his brother would never appoint Jackson.

"He said it would never happen....He killed it," Ettinger said, and Bedi agreed.

After five weeks of salty, f-bomb-laden testimony, it was hard to imagine revelations about Rod Blagojevich getting any more embarrassing.

But they did.

It was revealed that Blagojevich wangled an invitation to Obama's historic Election Day rally—but only by agreeing not to show up. And that the former governor once hid in the bathroom to avoid an uncomfortable encounter with the state's budget director. Most embarrassing, though, was what the former governor was heard on a recording saying about the people of Illinois: "Fuck all of you."

These revelations came through a secret recording and the testimony of Robert Greenlee, the Ivy League–educated former deputy governor under Blagojevich who testified that he was often dispatched to research job possibilities for Rod and Patti Blagojevich.

The morning of Election Day, Blagojevich went on a rant to Greenlee, mentioning a recent poll that showed he had a 13 percent approval rating. It was a slap in the face to Blagojevich, who fancied himself "the people's governor" and was especially proud of his healthcare initiatives and his efforts to increase access to public transit for the elderly.

"I fucking busted my ass and pissed people off and gave your grandmother a free fucking ride on a bus. OK? I gave your fucking baby a chance to have healthcare," Blagojevich is heard saying on tape. "And what do I get for that? Only 13 percent of you all out there think I'm doing a good job. So fuck all of you."

As this tape was played in the courtroom, Blagojevich grew flushed. To make matters worse, that same day, Blagojevich caught some flak trying to go to Obama's historic victory rally at Grant Park. When Blagojevich requested credentials, it put up red flags with the Obama camp, prompting an email from Obama staffer Anita Dunn that was forwarded to Greenlee.

The message: "WTF."

Greenlee explained that he had to practically beg Obama's people for an invite so that when the media asked Blagojevich if he got one, he didn't have to admit he got snubbed. Greenlee said he believed he won one, in part, because he "suggested" to Obama's people that Blagojevich wouldn't actually show. Blagojevich ultimately attended the rally but later is heard on a recording complaining that he wasn't really welcome. Greenlee testified that Blagojevich was in the office just two to eight hours a week and that Greenlee had to "trap him" to get him to sign bills.

"It was relatively difficult…because of a limited attention span," Greenlee said.

Once, Greenlee said, he joined the Blagojevich family at Southport Lanes restaurant and bowling alley, where they reviewed a stack of 20 pressing bills. Blagojevich vetoed some of the bills. Greenlee suggested that if he hadn't dined with the governor that night, some of the vetoed legislation would instead have been law. He also testified that he would say things to appease Blagojevich because the governor had a tendency to shut people out if he didn't like what they had to say. That included Blagojevich's budget director, John Filan. Greenlee said Blagojevich would hide in the bathroom, in the back of his office, or else would leave early to avoid Filan, who often brought him sobering news about the state's finances.

After six weeks of laying out evidence in Blagojevich's trial, the prosecution closed its case by revisiting an issue the former governor had always claimed was close to his heart: healthcare for kids.

Though the Senate seat scheming received the most attention, the allegation that the governor shook down a children's hospital was almost as startling. The CEO of Children's Memorial Hospital, Patrick Magoon, testified that about six days after Blagojevich promised him $10 million in state money for the hospital, he got a call from the then-governor's brother asking for a $25,000 campaign donation.

"I felt threatened, I felt at risk, and I felt a little angry," Magoon testified, closing out the government's case. In testimony, Magoon said it was clear that Blagojevich had sole discretion to give the hospital the money and that he had sole discretion to take it away.

"To receive a call within five or six days from his brother caused me great concern," Magoon said. "But what caused me the greatest concern was that the governor had the sole power" to release the money that would help pay for pediatric doctors who treat children at the hospital. "I felt the commitment could be rescinded," Magoon said. Magoon had testified that he headed a not-for-profit institution whose goal was to provide care to all kids. He said that for years he sought more state funding to help pay pediatric doctors, a challenge that left the hospital with a more than $20-million shortfall year after year.

The defense tried to convey to jurors that Magoon wasn't the victim he portrayed himself to be, as he made an annual salary and bonus that neared $1 million, and paid a lobbyist tens of thousands of dollars a month in fees. However, Judge Zagel blocked any details about Magoon's salary. The defense also pointed out that the state money did eventually go to the hospital, and it was used to give pediatric surgeons a raise.

On that same day, John Wyma finally took the stand, testifying under a grant of immunity.

Wyma said he sat in on a meeting in which Blagojevich discussed "getting Magoon for 50"—a reference to demanding $50,000 from the hospital CEO.

"It made me uncomfortable," Wyma said, eventually prompting him to withdraw from the governor's fundraising team. Wyma testified that in 2008 Blagojevich was floating fundraising plans that had Wyma growing "increasingly alarmed." The governor told Wyma he planned to withhold a multibillion-dollar roads project until he got $500,000 in fundraising from a road-building executive, Wyma testified.

Wyma also testified that he got a November 2008 phone call from Emanuel, who was acting as an emissary for Obama: "He said the president-elect would value and appreciate Valerie Jarrett in the Senate seat," Wyma said.

In his cross-examination, Sorosky painted Wyma as a money-hungry political insider who had his longtime friend Blagojevich to thank for his $1-million-plus lobbying income.

The prosecution rested.

Chapter Twelve

A One-Man Defense

On Monday, July 19, 2010, both brothers were scheduled to take the stand in their own defense. It was decided that Rob would go first. Before he took the stand, some members of the courtroom gallery could be heard whispering to each other, "I feel sorry for him" and "He got dragged into this."

Three months after he took over his brother's campaign fund, Rob Blagojevich said, he was approached with an offer by Nayak: Blagojevich would get $6 million in campaign money if he appointed Jesse Jackson Jr. to the Senate seat.

The offer came at an October 31, 2008, meeting. Nayak promised that if Jackson were appointed, $1 million would be raised for Blagojevich by the end of 2008 and then another $5 million would go to Blagojevich after Jackson became senator. Rob's testimony supported what Nayak had told authorities in his interview. Rob then testified that three days earlier, Bedi had told him of a $1.5-million offer for Jackson's appointment. He relayed the information from Bedi to his brother.

"We thought it was just a joke," Rob testified of Bedi's overture. "It was outrageous." Rob added that he didn't think he ever even relayed Nayak's $6-million offer to his brother. "We [had] dealt with the issue on the 28th," Rob Blagojevich told his lawyer, Michael Ettinger. "It was dead."

Rob testified that he hadn't known that Children's Memorial Hospital and the Maywood Park racetrack were awaiting state action when he discussed fundraising. His testimony in part served to explain phone calls regarding the Senate seat, including one on December 4, 2008, in which Blagojevich told him to approach Nayak and tell him Jackson would be elevated: "If there's tangible political support like you've said, start showing us now."

Rob testified that he got the call from his brother while he was at Starbucks on a rare outing with his wife, Julie, and was only half paying attention.

"I thought he was being rude. He knew I was with Julie," Rob said. He said he wasn't exactly sure what his brother meant by "tangible political support." He said he did set up a meeting with Nayak, and that after a newspaper article was published reporting that Blagojevich may have been captured on a wire, he postponed the meeting.

"Did you intend at any time to bring up fundraising with Raghu Nayak when you met him?" Ettinger asked.

"No," Rob replied.

Before getting started in his job as head of the Blagojevich campaign fund, Rob testified, he met with his brother's general counsel, Bill Quinlan, to go over the rules of fundraising.

"The bottom line," Rob Blagojevich testified that Quinlan told him, was to never condition a donation on governmental action.

"I was told never to tie the two," he said. "And I never did."

Rob was convincing on direct examination. Next was cross-examination by Niewoehner, who tore into the pristine image Ettinger had created. Rob stumbled as Niewoehner asked about a tape that hadn't been played—a November 5, 2008, discussion. "If you can get Obama to get Fitzgerald to close the investigation on you, it completely provides you with total clarity," Niewoehner quoted Rob telling his brother. Rob testified that this exchange had nothing to do with Jarrett's appointment and that it was instead meant "in the context of what politicians do." He seemed caught off guard, though, and the tension in the courtroom was palpable. If the prosecution could do this to Rob in less than 15 minutes, what would they do to his brother?

The session was brief and was to continue the next day. Rob worked with Ettinger to sharpen his testimony that night. His brother, meanwhile, huddled with his own legal team at home. He had been prepping with various defense lawyers for weeks to take the witness stand. The lawyers had complained that Blagojevich couldn't give an answer that took less than 15 minutes. They feared he wouldn't hold up to cross-examination. They urged him not to take the stand.

Blagojevich wasn't an easy sell. The team camped in his Ravenswood Manor home until the early hours of the morning. Blagojevich wrestled with the decision, arguing with Sam Adam Sr., who ultimately talked him out of it.

By the next morning, Rob had regrouped. He was a different man on the witness stand. He and Niewoehner became entrenched in a long back-and-forth over Rob's phone records on December 4, 2008, the day of a key phone call between the brothers about the Senate appointment. Prosecutors were trying to show that Rob was, in fact, actively trying to get ahold of his brother that day— suggesting maybe he wasn't as distracted as he'd claimed when the two had that critical conversation about Jackson.

"If you're trying to make the point that I was dying to talk to my brother, that's not the case," Rob said almost angrily, causing a ripple of giggles through the courtroom.

As he introduced the exhibits showing the calls, Niewoehner read aloud Rob's phone number. Rob reprimanded the prosecutor.

"Thank you for telling everyone my phone number," he snapped. That got a hearty laugh from the courtroom.

At one critical point, Niewoehner returned to something Rob had said the first day of the trial—that Rob didn't know what his brother meant when he said on tape he wanted "tangible, political support" from Jackson. Niewoehner asked Rob if he understood it now.

"You can split hairs," Rob said, sounding frustrated. "I do eventually accept the fact that he may be referring to fundraising." This was a major admission and a change of strategy from the day before. Ultimately, it appeared his defense believed it was better to admit that this indeed had been fundraising talk. At one point, with the jury out, Rob sat down in the witness chair and placed a yellow sticky note with his own writing on it on the podium in front of him. One of the government agents noticed it there and told Ettinger he wasn't allowed to have notes with him, and to get it out of there. Ettinger walked over to Rob and read the note, removed it, then stuck it to the middle of his own forehead and walked back toward the government team, mocking them. The note read "Stay focused!"

Rob was a new man, appearing much more at ease in the witness chair. He at times attempted to take control of the questioning from Niewoehner. The prosecution portrayed him as a willing participant in a scheme to wrest money from Nayak. Rob shrugged off that accusation by telling jurors he never took Jackson's emissary seriously when Nayak boasted he could mine that much money from Chicago's Indian-American community and from a "billionaire cousin" whom Nayak touted as a potential donor.

"Raghu Nayak is a very nice man. And he's prone to exaggerate," said Rob. He characterized Nayak's pledge as "outrageous," "naive," and borne of a "Keystone Cops" mentality. "He's a likable exaggerator, and I put that in context. I had no expectation of anything out of his 'billionaire cousin.' None."

Using the word "bribe," Niewoehner asked about Nayak's $6-million offer for the Senate seat

"I felt he was out of his element in what he was talking about, and I didn't hold it against him. Having grown up in an ethnic family," said Rob, who is Serbian-American, "I can see how they're very clumsy. That's just how I viewed the Indians—very awkward and clumsy and naive in our political system. And I put Nayak at the top of the chart." Rob moved to bolster his credibility by interjecting other examples of "outrageous" requests he received, and turned away, as Blagojevich's chief fundraiser. One instance involved a doctoral candidate willing to make what he described as a "substantial contribution" for help getting a PhD from a state university, a cash offer that the campaign rejected.

"I have another one, if you want to hear it," he continued, appearing to catch the prosecutor off guard. Niewoehner permitted him to launch into an anecdote about a meeting with a group of Greek-American restaurateurs from the northwest Chicago suburbs, who offered to hold a fundraiser for Blagojevich. Rob testified that when he met with the group to plan the event, they instead pulled out an architectural drawing of an access road they wanted built off a state highway to improve traffic to their businesses.

"It was egregious," Rob said on the stand, seeming to enjoy the retelling. "I said, 'I don't do that. I can't help you with that.' And as a result, they canceled the fundraiser." Niewoehner then asked Rob whether he chose to "contact law enforcement" about the exchange.

"I did not," he answered. But he rounded out his testimony by insisting he "never mixed" fundraising and government action.

Rob left the stand, and everyone prepared for the main event. This would be the moment Rod Blagojevich had been talking about since 2008—his chance to tell his side of the story from the witness stand. The jury was dismissed, and a sidebar was called.

In a sidebar with just attorneys and the judge, defense lawyers told the judge that it was Blagojevich's intention not to testify after all. Blagojevich sat at the defense table during this conference. Prosecutor Reid Schar, arms folded, leered at the defendant from across the room. In an environment where most things are tightly scripted, Blagojevich's flip-flop on testifying was a complete shock to the prosecution. Zagel told everyone to think about it that night and come back the next morning with a final decision.

After court that day, Rob walked downstairs looking as if a weight had been lifted off him. Though closing arguments hadn't even happened, there was a feeling that day that Rob had likely beaten the charges. One reporter asked what advice he would give his brother on whether to testify.

"Who am I to give him advice?" Rob answered, acknowledging that his relationship with his brother was "strained."

"He doesn't listen to me, you should know that by now," he said. "I told the truth, and if the truth is good, I did well."

Another reporter asked if he had any more plans to work in politics.

"I just want to go home to Nashville."

The next day, Judge Zagel had the jury taken out of the room, and then addressed Blagojevich. He explained to the former governor that it had to be his own decision not to testify.

"So now I'm going to ask you if it is your personal decision not to take the witness stand," Zagel said.

"Yes, Judge," the ex-governor responded.

Zagel asked Blagojevich if he had discussed the matter with his attorneys.

"Yes, Judge, fully and completely," he replied. And you have "deliberated in your own mind" after talking with your lawyers? the judge asked. "It is my decision, Judge, on the advice of my attorneys," Blagojevich said. "I made the decision freely and voluntarily."

Zagel called a break.

Blagojevich stayed in the courtroom and, in moments, dropped the serious face he had put on for Zagel. To the amazement of many in the room, he began signing autographs. At one point, Blagojevich propped one foot on a courtroom bench to continue signing, resting pieces of paper on his knee. Court security eventually asked him to stop.

When court resumed, Blagojevich's defense rested. It rested without calling a single witness, and despite his repeated public pleas to "play all the tapes," the ex-governor's team ultimately played not a one.

The pundits believed the decision not to testify greatly wounded Blagojevich's case with the jury. Here he had traveled the country appearing on news shows, and had even appeared on a reality TV show. In the courtroom, though, he wouldn't take the stand under oath? Even after his lawyer had promised jurors it would happen?

Afterward, Blagojevich told reporters, "Sam Adam Jr. still, to this moment, wanted me to testify, and frankly so did I...but ultimately I relied on the judgment and the advice of Sam Adam Sr., who is the coach of our team. After 39 years of experience, when he sat in my living room until 11:30 Monday night, after talking about these issues right after the government rested their case... Sam Adam Sr.'s most compelling argument, and ultimately the one that swayed me, was that the government in their case proved my innocence, they proved I did nothing illegal, and there was nothing further for us to add."

Blagojevich concluded, "I've learned a lot of lessons from this whole experience and perhaps maybe the biggest lesson I've learned is that I talk too much."

With closing arguments about to start, Annie and Amy Blagojevich accompanied their parents to the federal courthouse, where they had a front-row seat to prosecutors skewering their father. The younger of the Blagojevich daughters, seven-year-old Annie, spent much of the time on her mother's lap, flashing occasional smiles at the chalk drawings being produced by several nearby courtroom sketch artists.

Niewoehner outlined the charges for jurors. He repeatedly underscored the fact that evidence showing Blagojevich attempted to get something in exchange for official action was a violation of the law. It didn't matter that Blagojevich didn't get what he sought. "The law doesn't require you to be a successful crook, it just requires you to be a crook," Niewoehner told jurors.

The government's statements, though, ended up getting overshadowed by a battle that erupted later in the day. Sam Adam Jr., frustrated by Zagel's rulings repeatedly going against the defense, took on the judge, threatening not to follow them in his closing, which was scheduled for the next day.

With the jury out of the room, Zagel told Adam he didn't understand the law. He warned, "You will follow this order, because if you don't you will be in contempt of court."

After court, Adam said he would go to jail "in a heartbeat."

"I have no qualms of going to prison if that's what's best," he said. Adam argued that he should be able to tell jurors that the government mentioned 35 people in its case—including Rezko and serial swindler Stuart Levine—but never called them as witnesses. "You cannot draw an evidentiary inference from the fact a witness was not called by the other side when you had an equal right to call them," Zagel told Adam.

Adam's father whispered something to him, and the younger Adam stepped before Zagel.

"With all due deference to the court, I have a man here who's arguing for his life....I can't effectively represent this man....I can't follow this order," Adam told Zagel. "I'm willing to go to jail on this."

Tension fell over the courtroom as Adam's statement began. But throughout, Adam toed the line set by Zagel.

As in his opening statement, he alternately yelled and whispered. He paced throughout the room. He made jurors double over in laughter one minute—and attempted to draw outrage the next.

"They arrested Rod Blagojevich," he said. "You know who didn't get arrested? Jesse Jackson Jr."

He started by taking the heat for not making good on his promise that the former governor would take the stand. The trial had taken about eight weeks. That was much faster than anyone—including the defense—had anticipated.

"I gave you my word, and I meant every word of it," Adam told the jury. "I had no idea, no idea that in two months of trial [the government] would prove nothing."

Adam's 80-minute argument was a roller coaster. The prosecution objected more than 30 times. Zagel upheld every objection.

Adam cast his client as an insecure man who couldn't stop talking.

"If you had Joan and Melissa Rivers in a room, you wouldn't hear that much talk," Adam yelled, drawing laughter in the courtroom. "That's just the way he is."

He also made it clear that Blagojevich didn't always have the best ideas—including his considering Oprah Winfrey for the Senate.

"No one will say he is the sharpest knife in the drawer," Adam said.

As for the plot to sell the Senate appointment, what the government captured on the tapes wasn't "extortion" but "negotiation," Adam argued. Adam said Blagojevich dangled the appointment of Jesse Jackson Jr. in front of the White House because he knew Obama didn't want Jackson. The hope was that in return for appointing the preferred Lisa Madigan, Blagojevich would get some presidential help with advancing his bills through Madigan's father.

"If that ain't negotiation…you start high, and you go low," Adam said. "You can infer from those tapes whether or not he's trying to extort the president of the United States. That's an insecure man. He was just talking, he wasn't trying to extort."

At one point, the bombastic attorney launched into a story he said described his "Italian grandmother," saying she shot a mule dead after it stumbled three times. "That'sa one! That'sa two! That'sa three!" Adam yelled—really yelled—while mimicking the accent. When her husband called her stupid for shooting the mule, she warned him, "That'sa one!" When the punch line came, Adam's voice swelled to a fever pitch, prompting Schar to leap out of his chair and declare the display "inappropriate."

"I think they're objecting because it's beginning to look more like a show," Judge Zagel dryly cautioned Adam. He added that was "advice" and not a ruling.

A year later, Adam admitted the obvious about the mule story— it had been used before. (And no, his grandmother was not Italian.) People in the courtroom were confused by the analogy, but Adam's "mule story" would go down in courthouse lore.

"He's broke, man, BROKE! When I say broke, I mean BROKE!" Adam said of Blagojevich. Adam brought up that Blagojevich paid $500,000 in federal taxes while he was governor. *That* was really his main expenditure during those years—a fact the government failed to tell the jury, Adam said.

"He's paying for his own prosecution!" Adam screamed, pointing to the prosecution table. "This is crazy!"

As Adam continued, the prosecution continued objecting. After he had notched his eighth objection in 20 minutes, there was a moment of silence while he hung his head. The judge told him not to refer to prosecutors directly.

"OK. Forget who wrote the indictment," Adam said before starting his next question. Prosecutors Schar and Niewoehner, not looking at each other, shook their heads in unison.

Adam turned to prosecutors' claims that Patti had accepted kickbacks from Tony Rezko without doing any work. But she did do work, he argued.

"Kickbacks for work is a job, man!" he shouted, getting chuckles across the courtroom. He stretched, pointing across the room at Patti, who was wearing a white blouse and sitting in the front bench.

Prosecutors were rising to object every few minutes, and Zagel was sustaining them all. Adam played this to his advantage. He mocked the prosecutors and Zagel alike, making it appear exactly how he had wanted: that the judge and the prosecution were equally against him—and Blagojevich. At times, Adam faced jurors, not even looking at the prosecution table, and gestured his hand toward the prosecution—predicting, correctly, that they would stand up to object. He teased, saying one word at a time and looking at the prosecution, wondering when they'd stand up.

At one point Adam referred to "everyone in the whole world" knowing something, which notched an objection. Zagel reprimanded Adam for being so general. But Adam turned it around, making it seem the establishment was nitpicking at him. He told the jury sarcastically that he apologized if they thought he actually meant every single person in the whole world.

Adam clearly stunned at least one juror when he offered advice on what jurors should do if they were stuck in deliberations.

"Now, what would Sam say about this?" he said they should ask themselves.

Reid Schar followed Adam's animated statement, soberly summarizing one last time how the ex-governor cunningly used his state powers to enrich himself, and rebutting the notion that a "conspiracy of liars" somehow victimized Blagojevich. The ex-governor was a former prosecutor himself and could have immediately stopped the alleged extortion and bribery schemes designed to benefit him had he wanted to, Schar argued.

"Somehow he is the accidentally corrupt governor? I mean, come on. Come on," Schar told jurors, his voice rising. The prosecutor went on to ridicule the defense's assertion that Blagojevich fell victim to politics and liars and met his downfall through "one of the great frame-ups of all time." Ultimately, Schar said, enough evidence existed to convict Blagojevich and his brother on all counts. Doing so could undo some of the pain the ex-governor had inflicted upon the state.

"I don't know how you put a price on the damage Rod Blagojevich has caused," Schar said. "I know how you start to pay off the debt."

On July 29, 2010, as the six male and six female jurors began deliberations, they almost immediately had a question: Could they have a transcript of the government's closing argument? When the request was made known in open court, spectators took it as a sign that jurors had already sided with the government. This wasn't going to take long, observers thought. Since a closing argument is not evidence, the request was denied. On the third day of jury talks they had another request: "Is it permissible to obtain a transcript of the testimony? It would be helpful," the note read. They weren't allowed all of the testimony, but were told they could ask for more specifics later.

Then the days wore on, and the jurors were silent. With every day that passed, the prosecution's hopes dropped, and the defense's expectations climbed. Finally, on day 12 of talks, the jury revealed a whopper: they were deadlocked. "We have reached unanimous agreement on two counts. We have been unable to agree on any of the remaining counts," the jury note said.

Upon hearing the news, Blagojevich pressed his lips together and looked as if he were trying to suppress a smile. It was an ominous sign to prosecutors. The jury's struggles didn't square with the open-and-shut case prosecutors promised 19 months earlier when they arrested a sitting governor in his home and accused him of presiding over a "political crime spree" laid out in secret FBI wiretaps.

Meanwhile, inside the jury room, things couldn't have been more divided. One juror, JoAnn Chiakulas, did not believe the government had proved its case beyond a reasonable doubt. She refused to back down. As she dug in, other jurors squabbled with her. The women on the jury began feeling some of the men were trying to intimidate Chiakulas. This divided the group even more. Finally, on day 14 of talks, one of the jurors asked the judge to send back a script of the oath all the jurors took. He wanted to read it to Chiakulas. Finally, later that day, all parties were summoned to court. Judge Zagel entered the courtroom. The six alternate jurors who were dismissed at the beginning of the deliberations were seated in the courtroom, opposite the jury box. They had previously asked to be present for the verdict's reading. FBI chief Rob Grant and U.S. Attorney Patrick Fitzgerald were also seated in the courtroom gallery.

Rod Blagojevich was seated, looking at his lawyers, hands clasped, fingers drumming. Rob just leaned over to his wife, put his hands on hers, and whispered something reassuring. She nodded.

The jury found Rod Blagojevich guilty on just one of the 24 corruption counts against him—count 24, making false statements to the FBI. That count alleged that Blagojevich lied to federal agents in 2005 when they questioned him about "pay-to-play" politics. He told the agents he kept his fundraising and politics separate. It was considered the weakest charge of the lot, carrying a maximum five-year prison term and $250,000 fine. This meant the jury was divided on all 23 remaining counts against the ex-governor, and on all four counts against his brother. The judge declared a mistrial on the remaining counts where the jury said it was deadlocked.

"It is absolutely my intention to retry this...as quickly as possible," Schar said.

When the verdict was read, there wasn't a visible sense of relief at the defense table. Blagojevich looked at the jury and shook his head. It appeared the defense had been hoping for some acquittals. After the jury left, Sam Adam Jr. sat next to Blagojevich and put his arm around him, looking as if he were consoling him.

He hadn't been found guilty. But something else had dawned on him: he had to go through all of this all over again.

The government chalked up their lack of a win to a "holdout juror."

Chiakulas didn't like that characterization. She described herself as a "critical thinker" in an interview with WLS-TV's Paul Meincke.

"I seriously thought that I would be objective....It was really complicated," she said. "I didn't see a clear path to 'guilty' on some of the charges. Basically, I just didn't think the prosecution proved its case."

Chiakulas said she was under enormous pressure to give in, but "I would not have been able to live with myself" if she had gone along with others.

The decision leveled an embarrassing blow to the prosecution. The *Wall Street Journal* called for Fitzgerald's resignation. Sam Adam Jr. erroneously pegged the cost of a retrial at $30 million, denouncing prosecutors for wasting taxpayer money.

Prosecutors responded in writing. In a 34-page court filing, they complained that the Adams' statements to the media included made-up numbers and outright lies, all parts of an effort to speak to the next jury. Prosecutors wrote that the $30-million sum mentioned by Adam Jr. nearly equaled the annual budget of the U.S. Attorney's office, including rent, civil cases, and salaries and expenses of more than 150 non-Blagojevich prosecutors. "The defense's estimated cost of retrial is preposterous," prosecutors wrote.

They also responded to on-air statements by Blagojevich and by the Adams that prosecutors should turn their efforts to drug dealers and gangbangers, saying these were just a way for the ex-governor to deflect guilt.

"The notion that the government should forego prosecution of a corrupt ex-governor is offensive to any sense of justice," prosecutors wrote.

The U.S. Attorney's office couldn't relent. The FBI had arrested a sitting governor at his home, after all. If Blagojevich wasn't tried again, it would forever hurt the credibility of the office. But the office, the FBI, and the U.S. postal inspectors and IRS agents who worked the case all had great faith in their evidence.

After getting feedback from jurors, the trial team retooled its efforts. Just weeks after the mistrial in August 2010, prosecutors did something significant—they dropped charges against Rob. The jury was overwhelmingly against convicting Rob; those who did think he was guilty didn't think it was worth retrying him. The government believed that in strategic terms, having a more focused prosecution with fewer charges and without charges against Rob would go a long way in making the charges stick. In another strategic move, they also dropped the racketeering charges. Prosecutors became concerned after jurors told them the jury instructions on racketeering were too confusing. To prosecutors, what was now important was securing a conviction. To do that, they were convinced, they simply needed to focus their efforts. They worked to highlight their best evidence: Blagojevich's own words.

Chapter Thirteen

Retrial

Over the next several months, it became clear the former governor had replayed his first trial in his mind again and again, citing different witnesses, different lines of questioning. He became a man obsessed. He even tried convincing people in private settings who weren't party to his case of his innocence.

Blagojevich kept a slightly lower profile in late 2010 and early 2011 leading up to his second trial, which was scheduled for April 2011. He dug in and actually reviewed the case himself. His strategy with the media changed this time around. He granted interviews to print media, including the local papers.

In an interview inside his home on April 19, 2011, Blagojevich said he felt no elation when jurors in his first trial returned hung on 23 out of the 24 counts. He was still convicted of lying to the FBI.

"I felt, this is what happens when you don't put on a defense," he said. "The false statement conviction pissed me off, bothered me; it's not true."

Blagojevich alternated from self-deprecating and funny to dark and angry in this interview, especially if pressed about things he'd said that were caught on government recordings. His face would tighten. About the recordings, he asked, "You mean lawful conversations I had in the privacy of my home?"

His wife was in the house with him, appearing relaxed. Wearing jeans, she brought over cups of coffee.

"I'll confess to this: I have my moments of fear," Blagojevich admitted in a less guarded moment. "Especially late at night, when it's dark out—the witching hour—and your mind races and you ask yourself: 'How did this even happen?' I'm honestly talking, over and over again, time and time again to try to make the right decision."

Blagojevich had repeatedly criticized the government for not playing all the tapes, but in that same home interview, he conceded that he could control that himself—by taking the witness stand. Judge Zagel said he'd have more freedom to play recordings if Blagojevich took the stand.

The governor seemed poised to take the stand in the second trial, but this time, he didn't promise that he would. His retrial meant a new team. Sam Adam Jr. and Sam Adam Sr. had left the case. Now, Aaron Goldstein stepped up to take the lead, with Sorosky helping steer things, attorney Lauren Kaeseberg writing all the motions, and attorney Elliott Riebman also helping. The same team of prosecutors returned, but they reshuffled, giving the opening statements to Christopher Niewoehner. The prosecution's case was largely on autopilot. It was a more focused case than in the previous trial, with fewer witnesses and fewer charges. The big difference this time would be with the defense.

The defense witnesses were few, but they were an all-star cast. Jesse Jackson Jr., a sitting congressman, and Rahm Emanuel, now the sitting mayor of Chicago, were each called briefly. Emanuel's testimony was over in a matter of minutes. Jackson's, however, was an event. The congressman settled into the witness chair, and with much animation, steadfastly denied making any quid pro quo offers. He wasn't pressed—either by prosecutors or the defense—about his discussions with Nayak.

Jackson turned out to be a disaster for the defense. He mocked Blagojevich and appeared to be enjoying it. He also leveled an allegation against the ex-governor: Jackson claimed that Blagojevich tried to extort a $25,000 campaign contribution from him. When he didn't pay up, Jackson said, Blagojevich punished him by passing over Sandi Jackson for a position with the Illinois Lottery.

"I walked in the room and there was a chill in the air. I could see in his face he wasn't going to be able to do anything for Sandi," Jackson said. "The governor came up to me and said, 'I'm sorry the thing with Sandi didn't work out.'"

Then Jackson dropped the kicker: "In classic Elvis Presley fashion, he snapped his fingers and said, 'You should have given me that $25,000.'"

Jackson later did his best Elvis impression, drawling "thank you very much" and repeatedly snapping his fingers while looking toward Blagojevich. The courtroom gallery and jurors laughed.

It was time for Goldstein's redirect examination on his own witness, but it felt more like cross-examination. He told Jackson he was not a big fan of Elvis. Jackson snapped, "You work for someone who is," winning some groans from the gallery. Blagojevich had his mouth agape during some parts of the testimony. He shifted in his chair, flushed, shook his head, and smiled, he would later say, in disappointment.

"With regard to that other thing about Elvis, all I can tell you is that it's absurd, it's not true, it didn't happen," Blagojevich said later.

After Jackson and Emanuel left the building and the excitement over their testimony had died down, lawyers prepared for their marquee witness. On May 26, the defense called Rod R. Blagojevich.

Upon hearing his name, Blagojevich stood up, buttoned his jacket, walked over to Patti and kissed her on the head, and then made the walk across the courtroom. After taking an oath and settling into his chair, the man who needed no introduction introduced himself.

"I'm Rod Blagojevich," he said, looking at the jury. "I used to be your governor, and I'm here today to tell you the truth."

Blagojevich told the jury he would get into talking about his tapes later. But first he took a moment to apologize for profane utterances on tape that jurors had been listening to for weeks, and the public had heard for more than three years.

"When I hear myself saying that on tape, I'm an effin' jerk, and I apologize," he said. "It makes you wince." The former governor told the courtroom that his teenage daughter, Amy, told him that morning to watch his language when she wished him good luck on the stand.

The fact that he started with an apology made many wonder where his testimony would lead. What would he say about the schemes captured on the tapes? Would he reveal anything new? Would he admit to some of the charged crimes? Did his political enemies have anything to worry about?

It turned out that as far as substance was involved, the crowd would have to wait. As the long-winded speeches grew increasingly protracted, the excitement and anticipation in the room—in the entire building—slowly dissipated.

Under questioning by Aaron Goldstein, Blagojevich went deep into his personal history, from Little League to his love for Elvis to growing up with immigrant parents. Blagojevich launched into a tale about how his Serbian immigrant father influenced him.

"He came to this whole new place and had to start over. For better or worse, I think I picked up my dad's propensity to dream," Blagojevich said. He tried to draw a parallel between himself and his father, who fought the Nazis in World War II. He said his dad didn't take other people's advice.

"Listening to the advice of someone is a mixed blessing, as I certainly have learned," Blagojevich said, likely implying that as governor, his advisers led him astray. This was a defense alluded to several times during cross-examination of government witnesses. Here, Blagojevich appeared to choke up when he explained that his parents had both passed away.

"I've always felt, always felt that my parents...helped me from heaven, just sort of helped guide me," he said, pointing up. He described a moment when he "thought politics was a safe profession," earning a big smile from a juror. He talked about transferring to Northwestern University for his final two years of college. He said he was insecure, and he called that insecurity a "tremendous flaw."

"I always felt that these kids at Northwestern, they came from wealthier families, they came from better schools. I always felt a little intimidated that they were a lot smarter than me," he said. "I was afraid that I wouldn't measure up to the other kids." While other students were walking around in khakis and shirts with crocodiles on them, he said he was still in the "age of polyester."

"It was right out of *Saturday Night Fever*," he said. "You are what you are, but I started wearing less polyester."

To say Blagojevich's testimony meandered would be an understatement. Whether the prosecution liked it or not, Blagojevich was taking the courtroom audience on an in-depth biographical tour of his life, with Goldstein acting as his character foil. Blagojevich had no shortage of material. "Just as an aside..." he'd say again and again as he digressed onto another topic. He dove into his love for history and reading.

"I had a man-crush on Alexander Hamilton," Blagojevich said at one point, drawing snickers. He went on about his Shakespeare class and about his poor performance on the LSAT—he was under the 50th percentile both times he took the test to get into law school, he said.

He talked about his Serbian name, Milorad, which means "happy worker." He recalled his days as a college student and just after: "Those were the days when your hairbrush was an extension of your hand." All along, he appeared fully aware of the jurors. He'd direct comments their way, look over, smile. He didn't get anything back.

It was typical for Blagojevich to spend several minutes answering one question. He went on at length so often that at one point he cut himself off and asked Goldstein: "Do you want to ask the questions?" At that, Reid Schar raised his eyebrows, seemingly in agreement.

Eventually, Goldstein asked Blagojevich about Lon Monk. It was a red-hot sore point for Blagojevich that Monk, once a dear friend, had helped the government in the case against the ex-governor. Monk and Blagojevich met each other while traveling abroad for law school. Blagojevich said he had recognized Monk as a fellow student from Pepperdine while touring London on a double-decker bus.

"It didn't take long while we were there in London, what was the beginning of a lifelong, very close friendship," Blagojevich said. One bonding interest was the two men's love of running. On the stand, Blagojevich admitted to having "a certain narcissism" when it came to his passion for staying in shape. He talked about how he nearly failed out of law school and kept it a secret from everyone but his family. But one day, he told Monk.

"Those are the kind of little things that bond you with someone," he said. "There are friends that you love in a real friend way, not in a, you know what I'm talking about. I love Lon. That's why he was so important to me, that's why he was at my wedding." He trusted Monk "infinitely," he said.

During the lengthy testimony, one juror appeared annoyed. One held her hand on her chin, appearing to concentrate steadily. Another fought to keep her eyes open. Only one took copious notes.

Blagojevich had begun talking about his fledgling legal career when he suddenly brought his testimony to a halt. He said he was working in a law office when, one day, he met his future wife, Patti. But he never quite got her name out. Blagojevich couldn't speak; he pointed to his wife, sitting diagonally from him, and struggled to talk.

All eyes turned to Patti. Red-faced, she burst into tears.

"And…*scene*," a female TV reporter whispered.

Patti's brother, Richie, passed his hand over his sister's back.

"Let's take a break," said Judge Zagel.

"Oh no, I'm good, Judge, I'm fine," Blagojevich protested. But Zagel adjourned for lunch.

Before the jury was back, prosecutors complained about Blagojevich's long-winded answers.

"In an effort, and only an effort to move things along," Schar said Blagojevich should answer in a way that's "maybe more focused and responsive to the actual questions."

"It's fine," Zagel said. "This is the chance for him to tell his story." Zagel did make clear that once they entered into substantive questions about the charges, Blagojevich would have to cut the narrative.

It was around this point in the trial that Blagojevich did something unwittingly that perhaps would have saved him if he had done it in 2008—he made himself inaudible. The whole trial was put on pause as his microphone on the witness stand appeared to malfunction. "It's not my fault," he declared of the technical difficulties. Turns out it was. The ex-governor's binder was resting on the on/off switch. When told, he said, "I misspoke. Evidently it was my fault," to much laughter.

The ex-governor's tendency to micromanage—or obsess—came through during the questioning. Blagojevich started answering one of Goldstein's questions, but then stopped.

"Strike that," said Blagojevich, who the day earlier had told jurors he graduated from law school knowing little about the law. "Can I say 'Strike that'? Strike that."

Patti and the Blagojeviches' daughter Amy watched from the bench. At a morning break, Patti pulled out a laminated photograph of her late mother, Margaret Mell, and looked at it with her daughter. When the defense played its first tape, featuring Blagojevich speaking with legal adviser Bill Quinlan, the ex-governor's profane mouth surfaced: "Bullshit," Blagojevich was heard telling Quinlan. Patti looked at her daughter and smiled.

Patti was mentioned on the stand again, too: Blagojevich described, in his testimony, he got into politics in the first place as a ploy to win her over. Her father asked him if he was willing to dabble in politics by running for state representative. "You interested in running, Blagojevich?" he said Mell asked him. "Her dad liked me," Blagojevich said. "I had a better shot with Patti." He had a question for Mell: "Am I free to make my own decision on the issues?" Mell responded, according to Blagojevich, "I don't give an F."

Despite the occasional telling moment of candor, however, Blagojevich continued to give detailed, often rambling answers to questions. On a break, Judge Zagel told Blagojevich and Goldstein that the narrative was risky. It's "for the benefit of your client to ask questions quickly," Zagel said, noting that if politicians hear dead air, they tend to fill it. "Because he's pretty much giving you the chance to ask him another question," Zagel continued.

At one point, as Blagojevich rambled on, a reference to actor Larry David caused Schar to stand up to object.

"I knew that was going to happen," Blagojevich quipped, causing an aggravated Schar to sit down, head in hands.

On May 31, 2011, Blagojevich attorney Lauren Kaeseberg complained that the prosecutors—who directly faced the jurors—were making faces as the ex-governor spoke on the stand. Kaeseberg said prosecutors were also having "animated discussions" in front of the jury during Blagojevich's testimony.

"We just ask that they stop making faces while he's testifying," Kaeseberg said. Schar said the team did confer before making objections, but he didn't think they were making faces.

"We'll be mindful," Schar said. "I don't think that's the case." Zagel said he hadn't noticed anything but that "I'll watch the government very carefully."

Goldstein ran through the various schemes floated on the recordings, and the ex-governor denied them all. He didn't shake down Rahm Emanuel's brother, Ari. Nor did he try to extort Johnny Johnston. He didn't take bribes from Rezko, nor did he meet with Kelly, Rezko, and Monk in California and discuss profiting from state deals while he was in office. The topic of the ethics legislation, which was pending in 2008, came up. This was a sensitive issue that the defense knew it had to handle with just the right touch. The feds inferred that much of Blagojevich's motive to inappropriately squeeze donors for campaign money stemmed from the pending passage of this bill. The bill would have banned the governor from taking money from people doing business with the state.

Blagojevich admitted he was intensely interested in keeping the campaign fund flush.

"If you're in a strong political position, it gives you the independence to, frankly, lose friends...and even lose political allies," Blagojevich said. Prosecutors said Blagojevich knew he could no longer take donations from contractors by the end of that year because of that bill. So they alleged that Blagojevich had ramped up his shakedown schemes.

Blagojevich said he saw it a different way. It was still legal to seek campaign contributions until the end of the year. He said he wanted to kill that bill in favor of another bill that had more extensive legislative reforms, forcing lawmakers also to abide by the same rules as the governor. He claimed that Emil Jones, who had at the time been Illinois state senate leader, agreed with him. That is, until later in 2008, when "a sheepish Emil Jones" told Blagojevich he had to call the original ethics bill for a vote, at the request of Obama, who was running for president at the time.

Finally, Blagojevich began to tackle some of the charges against him, starting with the allegations that he held up legislation that benefited the horseracing industry in Illinois because he didn't get a campaign contribution from Johnny Johnston. Blagojevich said Johnston had promised him a $100,000 contribution early in 2008. He said he pressed Johnston to fulfill that commitment and that Monk was acting as the go-between.

"My understanding was that he [Johnston] was going to fulfill his commitment and that it was due to arrive sometime before the end of October," Blagojevich said. "That was, in my experience with the Johnstons [Johnston's father and brother were also involved in the industry], they always fulfilled their fundraising commitments in the past [sic]." The defense had been trying to make clear that the Johnstons had historically been campaign contributors, and that therefore it wouldn't be unusual for the governor to hit them up for money again.

Blagojevich said he wasn't holding up the bill. He was simply reviewing it.

"The legislature would sneak things into bills in the fine print that would undo the things you want to do," Blagojevich said, calling the language a "poison pill." Monk had testified earlier that it was his understanding that Blagojevich didn't sign the bill because Johnston didn't pay into the governor's campaign fund, but that morning, Blagojevich offered up a new, convoluted explanation for why he didn't sign the racing bill. It involved the late Chris Kelly.

Kelly, Blagojevich testified, was trying to get a presidential pardon for charges leveled against him in a federal indictment. To do that, he was using connections in Florida, who included the Johnston family, to try and get former Governor Jeb Bush to ask his brother George W. Bush for a presidential pardon.

"What [counsel Bill] Quinlan was telling me was that Chris was pressing him to get me to sign that bill and was angry that it hadn't been signed yet," Blagojevich said, referring to a conversation with his legal counsel. "It was a big, bold red flag to be very careful." Kelly had been indicted, and Blagojevich knew he was under federal scrutiny: "I was very aware that the ladies and gentlemen at that table were investigating me," he said, referring to prosecutors. That's why he didn't move on signing the bill, he said. The prosecution couldn't call Kelly to corroborate the theory, as by then Kelly had been dead for about eight months.

The proposed legislation siphoned profits from the competing casino industry and kicked them over to horseracing.

"Give us the fucking money, because it's $9,000 a day, for every day" that Blagojevich doesn't sign the bill, Monk had said in a recorded conversation.

While the feds contend this was another way that Blagojevich had tried to squeeze Johnston, the ex-governor said he didn't think Johnston's Maywood Park racetrack was really losing that money.

"I understood Monk to be spinning, giving the company line," he said.

Day three of testimony arrived, and the questioning eventually turned to the topic of Children's Memorial Hospital. Before the end of the lunch break, Blagojevich held court in the hallway, chatting it up with reporters and reflecting on his Northwestern days and Elvis Presley. Zagel, meanwhile, scolded Goldstein, telling him to keep his client on point during this session. Zagel told Goldstein he had to stop asking questions that invited long-winded answers. It had been fine to ask those questions earlier in Blagojevich's testimony, when the questions focused on Blagojevich's history. But not now.

Once things got going, Goldstein asked his client when he first heard of Children's Memorial. "On October 14, 1967," Blagojevich said, drawing sighs all around.

"Don't want to go that far back," Zagel said, appearing to wrestle with remaining restrained. Blagojevich then tried to slip in the fact that his cousin had died at Children's Memorial. Prosecutors quickly objected.

"Your Honor, it's relevant," Goldstein protested as he tried to ask Blagojevich what the hospital meant to him. "It's relevant to what their exact allegations are."

"What I'm concerned about has to do with the open invitation in your questions for a long, narrative answer," Zagel replied. "I really don't want another speech and it's not proper form." Blagojevich finally answered "yes" when Goldstein asked if it was fair to say his life experiences shaped his healthcare policies. Blagojevich eventually testified that he never shook down Patrick Magoon, the CEO of Children's Memorial Hospital, by holding up a promised increase in pay for pediatric doctors serving Medicaid patients while he waited for Magoon to hold a fundraiser for him, and never demanded or threatened that CEO.

Blagojevich gave his interpretation of what prosecutors pointed to as clear evidence that he had ordered a stop to the fee increase for Children's Memorial doctors. At issue was this November 12, 2008, recorded phone exchange with Deputy Governor Robert Greenlee:

> BLAGOJEVICH: And we have total discretion over it?
>
> GREENLEE: Yep.
>
> BLAGOJEVICH: So we could pull it back if we needed to, budgetary concerns, right?
>
> GREENLEE: We sure could. Yep.
>
> BLAGOJEVICH: OK, that's good to know.

Greenlee himself testified that in that phone call, he believed Blagojevich was giving him an order to halt the rate increase. He testified during the government's case that Blagojevich often gave him vague orders. For his part, Blagojevich said he was "absolutely not" ordering Greenlee to stop the rate increase, which was why at the end of the call he said "That's good to know." His explanation for the phone call was less conceivable than Greenlee's: Blagojevich said he was checking to see if it would be appropriate to call Patrick Magoon to ask for a fundraiser; Friends of Blagojevich was hoping to get $25,000 from a fundraiser they hoped Magoon would host.

"That was important to help me decide" if it would be OK to call Magoon, Blagojevich testified. He said he didn't want to make Magoon "uncomfortable" by hitting him up for campaign contributions if the increase was still pending, and didn't want Magoon to get the wrong idea.

"'That's good to know'; therefore, I'm not gonna call Patrick Magoon. I'm not gonna call and make him feel uncomfortable with this pediatric rate increase still hovering," Blagojevich testified. "It was a relief. I didn't want to call him anyway."

The Blagojevich testimony inched closer to the charge that he tried selling the vacant Senate seat. He listed off his advisers, some of whom had legal experience, and their extensive credentials (one, Blagojevich said, was valedictorian of his high school class; this anecdote prompted an exasperated Zagel to rub his eyes). The defense seemed to be attempting to show that Blagojevich didn't know that what he was doing was wrong, and was instead being encouraged by Chief of Staff John Harris and legal counsel Bill Quinlan.

After court, Zagel warned the defense team to reconsider a defense that Blagojevich was acting on bad legal advice when he allegedly sought to trade the Senate seat.

"I think it is better for the defense not to go down that road," Zagel said.

The defense at one point played its own tape referring to a *Chicago Tribune* article published on December 5, 2008, which said Wyma was cooperating with a federal investigation. In the recorded call, Blagojevich was heard saying he was still reeling from finding out Wyma was cooperating with the government.

"It was startling and shocking, and there's all kinds of emotions that go through your mind when you think about a friend that might have been doing that, not to mention it's frightening and terrifying," Blagojevich testified.

Finding out about the *Tribune* article helped Blagojevich recall an October 22 meeting where he remembered Wyma "seemed weird." That day, a *Tribune* reporter was also outside his campaign office.

"My mind began to reconstruct that day with this particular reporter and John Wyma," Blagojevich testified. He said he called Quinlan.

"My God, what could I have said?" Blagojevich testified as to what went through his mind. "Do you think I said something wrong? Could I have stumbled into crossing a line?"

Blagojevich closed the day by setting up the defense's response to the Senate seat allegations.

"I felt that the Senate seat was one of my last, best opportunities to try to use this opportunity to make the best decision I could, and I wanted to be very careful," he testified. To that end, he considered different options—"good ones, bad ones, stupid ones, ugly ones"—to try to make the best decision.

On June 1, the ex-governor's fourth day on the stand, the Blagojevich team was set to tackle the Senate seat issue. The defense had spent part of the prior weekend reworking its strategy. The week before, Zagel had ruled that Blagojevich could testify that he had really wanted to appoint Lisa Madigan to the Senate seat in exchange for support with his legislative agenda. But Zagel said the defense would likely not be permitted to any of the recordings that support the theory, because Judge Zagel didn't believe it. The defense repeatedly argued that the jury should be able to decide whether it was believable.

Beginning in the summer of 2008, Blagojevich testified, he was thinking that if he had the opportunity, he would appoint one of the following people to the Senate seat: Emil Jones; Lisa Madigan; Danny Davis; or himself. Appointing himself to the Senate was "never something I felt deep down comfortable with," Blagojevich testified. But he said that spending the remainder of his term as governor in his state's difficult political environment was an unappetizing prospect. By late October, he said, he was still considering the same candidates, with the inclusion of U.S. Rep. Luis Gutierrez.

Blagojevich then got to Jackson. He testified that he had received offers of fundraising support in exchange for the Senate seat from both Rajinder Bedi and Raghu Nayak, but that "I had no intention of appointing Congressman Jackson, with or without" the offers.

The case arrived at a pivotal point. Blagojevich wanted to testify that he didn't know that what he was doing with respect to the
Senate seat was wrong. Zagel allowed the defense to give him an
"offer of proof," which essentially involved the ex-governor testifying without the jury present.

Whether because it was from the heart, because it was the most
practiced, or because his main audience—the jury—was now ab-
sent, this portion of Blagojevich's testimony arguably came off as
the most candid statement he'd made thus far. It was certainly the
least labored. Blagojevich easily cited the historical precedents on
his mind when he sought an ambassadorship or a nonprofit post in
exchange for appointing Valerie Jarrett. President Ford had offered
Ronald Reagan two cabinet positions and an ambassadorship not
to run against him, Blagojevich said, and President Eisenhower
had offered Earl Warren a seat on the U.S. Supreme Court in exchange for his support. Blagojevich said he believed that trading
his power to appoint for a personal benefit was perfectly legal.

"Did you honestly believe that what you were talking about
was legal?" Goldstein asked without the jury present.

"Yes, I did," Blagojevich said.

"Did you honestly believe that exchanging the Senate seat for
[a cabinet post such as] Health and Human Services was legal?"
Goldstein asked.

"Yes, I did," Blagojevich said.

Or a nonprofit position or an ambassadorship?

"Yes," Blagojevich answered.

Why did he think it was legal? Blagojevich ticked off more political deals from U.S. history. According to Doris Kearns Good-
win's *Team of Rivals*, Abraham Lincoln made a deal with the governor of Pennsylvania to make him secretary of war in exchange
for his support for president, Blagojevich said. Blagojevich said
he believed Barack Obama and Hillary Clinton made a deal for

Obama's campaign to give $10 million to help her retire her campaign debt—and to appoint her U.S. Secretary of State—in exchange for her pulling out of the race for president. (Reports indicate that Obama didn't ask Clinton to be Secretary of State until after he was elected.) When President Kennedy gave up his Senate seat, Blagojevich said, he installed a placeholder figure there until his brother Ted was old enough to run for it. And when Blagojevich was in Congress, Henry Hyde, the former Judiciary Committee chair, asked him to support an Alabama judge's desire to post the Ten Commandments in his courtroom in exchange for Hyde approving a post office named for a slain police officer in Blagojevich's district.

Zagel was skeptical.

"His historical recitation involves some things historically accepted as true, some things [that are] speculative," he said. "The stuff about his experiences actually doing things in political life is not analogous to the issues we are dealing with here...It's just a bunch of irrelevant stuff."

Blagojevich kept mentioning that he discussed all of this with his senior advisers, including his general counsel, Quinlan.

"My desire was to comply with the law," Blagojevich said. "I was particularly careful, I thought. [I had] a full desire [that] whatever idea was brought to me, was discussed by all my senior advisors and Mr. Quinlan was among them. No one ever said, 'You can't do that—it was illegal.' I was determined to make sure I followed the law when I made my ultimate decision."

Prosecutors called that a backdoor attempt to introduce the argument that Blagojevich was not guilty because he was relying on the advice of counsel, an argument Zagel had already said he couldn't make. And Zagel was unconvinced.

"My ruling is: opinions about the legality of something are out," Zagel said. He also admonished Blagojevich's lawyers: "I don't want to see that by implication…He's perfectly free to say 'I thought it was OK to do this.'"

When the jury returned, they heard that Blagojevich talked to Quinlan three times a day, and they heard him deny that he ever shook someone down. But he couldn't explicitly say that he thought what he was doing was legal. That left Blagojevich to come up with other reasons as to why he was saying what he was on the tapes about trading the seat.

Blagojevich had long insinuated that there was more to the tapes than what the public was hearing—that portions of calls favorable to him might have been deleted. As his testimony unfolded, he made a similar suggestion in front of the jury. Zagel responded by sending the jury out of the room.

Zagel then turned to Blagojevich and his lawyers and said it was "entirely inappropriate" to make such a suggestion in front of the jury. Zagel said he had ruled on the same matter already since Blagojevich took the stand, and that now he saw the ex-governor as flagrantly violating his order.

"This is a deliberate effort by this witness to raise something that he can't raise, to [suggest] something that was good as eliminated," Zagel said. "This is not fair. This is a repeated example of a defendant who wants to say something [by] smuggling [it] in. He did that yesterday, day before yesterday. This is not right. I am going to give an instruction to the jury that he is not to refer to stuff that's been deleted on the witness stand in the presence of the jury.

"Do you understand what I have just said?" he asked, visibly irritated. "Is that clear?"

"It's clear," one of Blagojevich's lawyers, Lauren Kaeseberg, said in a similarly annoyed tone.

"Do you think it's possibly clear to your client?" Zagel answered.

"I'm sure it is," Kaeseberg replied.

An hour later, though, Zagel again cleared out the jury. He implored the defense to get control of its client.

"There are some things now that have been repeated for the 15th and 16th time," Zagel said. "There's a certain flavor of campaign speeches here." Zagel said he'd given the defense extraordinary leeway.

"I've permitted you to do something that's rarely done with a defendant in a criminal case. I've permitted you to lead him," Zagel said. "This repetitiveness will diminish the attentiveness of the jury." He suggested that the defense attorneys skip lunch and instead work with their client on giving more concise answers.

Blagojevich testified at one point that former Speaker of the House Dennis Hastert told him to get something for himself in exchange for the Senate seat.

"Get your quid pro quo and make it a twofer," Blagojevich alleged Hastert said to him. What Hastert meant, Blagojevich continued, was that he should appoint someone like Illinois Secretary of State Jesse White or Lisa Madigan—a state official—so he could also appoint a replacement for their positions, thus getting a "two-for-one" appointment. Blagojevich said he had a "very close relationship" with Hastert, whom he saw as a "seasoned veteran" and "the coach you wanted to always impress."

While discussing his November 2008 meeting with Tom Balanoff, Blagojevich explained that appointing Obama's apparent choice, Valerie Jarrett, seemed like a giveaway. Meanwhile, he said, he would be stuck back in Illinois with legislative leader Michael Madigan blocking his every move in the legislature. He felt this would only get worse if he didn't name Madigan's daughter to the seat.

"I'd be worse than a lame duck, because in addition to the existing gridlock, I wouldn't have made his daughter a senator" when he had the chance to, he said.

Eventually, Blagojevich got around to what he called the "phrase heard 'round the world": "I've got this thing and it's fucking golden, and I'm just not giving it up for fucking nothing." What did he mean by this?

Many observers might have expected Blagojevich's reply to be practiced. But he tripped over his words.

"Well, that's the, that's, uh, the Senate seat," Blagojevich stumbled. "I was saying that this opportunity is effin' golden and that's what I was saying, and I don't want to give it up for nothing, so we had these discussions."

Goldstein pressed: what did he *mean*?

"I'm afraid to answer this," Blagojevich responded. "I'd like to answer it. I'm not sure how to answer it....In my mind, I didn't know," Blagojevich said. "I had no idea, other than all these different ideas that we were throwing around, and I was trying to figure out what, if anything, could possibly be part of a deal for the Senate seat. And I didn't know and that's why I was talking about it."

Blagojevich tried to persuade the jury that in his taped conversation with Balanoff, he was not demanding one thing for another, but that he had "floated the idea" of getting a cabinet post as they discussed Jarrett's appointment.

Balanoff was, after all, the same man Obama had called and given the green light to talk to Blagojevich about appointing Jarrett to the U.S. Senate.

Blagojevich said that while talking to Balanoff, he hesitated and explained his own personal and political predicament if he appointed Jarrett and he got nothing.

"You all go to Washington, D.C., doing all this historic, beautiful stuff on healthcare and I'm left behind. I gotta consider those dynamics, too," Blagojevich said he told Balanoff, referring to the prospect of remaining in gridlocked Illinois politics while so many other leading figures in Illinois Democratic politics went to Washington. "He said he understood."

Then Blagojevich made the ask: Could he possibly get a cabinet position; specifically, could he be named to head up Health and Human Services?

"You could just see the embarrassment in his face," Blagojevich said of Balanoff. "'You have no chance at that. It's not going to happen for you.' I felt so uncomfortable for how he looked."

Blagojevich described the conversation as "a bad try." He denied ever pushing it further or saying he'd only appoint Jarrett if he got something in return.

"I did not want to convey a promise to Tom Balanoff...I floated the idea," Blagojevich said. "He was quick to honestly reject it as being unrealistic."

As the direct questioning wore on, it seemed Goldstein was trying to waste time in hopes that Blagojevich would have a three-day weekend to recuperate and prep for what promised to be a scathing attack by prosecutors. It was Wednesday, and the judge had announced a day off for that Friday. The ex-governor was clearly growing fatigued on the stand.

"I don't know what I'm saying. What am I talking about here?" Blagojevich asked Goldstein at one point. "Can you help me?"

At least half a dozen times that afternoon, Blagojevich asked Goldstein things like "Where are you?" or "Do you have a question for me?" or seemed to lose his train of thought.

On a break, Zagel scolded Goldstein.

"I do believe now...that you are trying to run the clock," he said after having dismissed the jurors. There was still one day left in the week.

The next morning, on Thursday, June 2, 2011, the prosecution was clearly growing antsy. Schar asked Zagel if the trial could be held the following Monday after all, instead of having the day off.

Zagel told Schar no, but suggested this instead: no matter what time the defense finished that day, the prosecution would have the option to begin its cross-examination.

The testimony went on. Blagojevich said he had talked to Rahm Emanuel about appointing Lisa Madigan and Emanuel seemed "pleasantly surprised" that he'd really consider her. Blagojevich continued that Doug Scofield and his other advisers were pushing him to exchange something for the Senate seat.

"[Scofield] was advising me to leverage it for whatever was most helpful to me," Blagojevich testified. "He was giving me his view on what my friends thought I should do with this, that I should leverage the Senate seat. Any decision I would ultimately make on the Senate seat had to be legal, obviously," Blagojevich said clearly and slowly into the microphone, leaning in. He glanced at the jury. The prosecution objected. Blagojevich wasn't allowed to bring up legality, and the judge upheld the prosecution's objection.

As Blagojevich ticked through his meandering thoughts regarding a series of recorded phone calls, Osama bin Laden's name came up. The courtroom visibly perked up. Blagojevich said that in 2008 he'd had discussions with advisers about appointing himself senator, then heading to Afghanistan and hunting down Osama bin Laden. The idea was so far-fetched that likely he mentioned it in an attempt to demonstrate the absurdity of the recorded discussions at the time. At this point, it seemed the defense had definitively jumped the shark.

It was the afternoon of June 2 when Blagojevich finally faced the most challenging allegation against him: that he planned to make a deal to get campaign donations in exchange for appointing Jesse Jackson Jr. He had to explain what seemed like damning tapes in which he was heard having his brother set up a meeting with Nayak.

He was not referring to the secret FBI wiretaps, he said, when he told his brother to assume "the whole world is listening."

"'The whole world is listening' is a phrase I use all the time," Blagojevich testified. "When you talk to someone...in politics... you assume everybody's listening." Blagojevich said he wanted Raghu Nayak to help broker a deal in which Jackson would agree to back a "mortgage foreclosure bill" that Blagojevich supported. The explanation quickly raised eyebrows. There was no mention anywhere on the recordings about a mortgage bill, making it seem as if this was a cover story the defense had concocted.

"In my mind, that day and the day before, we were working on a mortgage foreclosure bill that passed the Senate. In my mind that day was a desire to pass a mortgage foreclosure bill," Blagojevich said. "This wasn't even said because my words were outpacing my ideas."

Even after all these phone calls and arrangements to meet with a Jackson donor, Blagojevich testified, "I was never going to appoint Congressman Jackson."

Goldstein and Blagojevich then steered toward a recording made on December 8, 2008, the day before Blagojevich was arrested.

"Right now if I had to pick I'd say Gery Chico [the former Daley aide]. And we'd call him an Hispanic, right?" he says to his chief of staff John Harris. In the call, Blagojevich brings up the Lisa Madigan deal, saying he would like to tap Emanuel to construct such a deal.

"If you're picking today, who you picking?" Blagojevich asks Harris. "Do we ever make the move with Madigan, or do we forget the whole thing? The question is how do you do it? Get Rahm to go in."

Next, the defense played a different December 8 call. It happened at 8:43 p.m. Blagojevich was talking to Greenlee about how Emanuel had agreed to be a go-between and broker a deal with the Madigans to get the Illinois attorney general appointed to the Senate seat in exchange for support of a Blagojevich legislative package.

The last question from the defense was "Rod, were you arrested the next day?"

Blagojevich answered, "Yes."

That was it. It was time. The reason Blagojevich's lawyers urged him against taking the stand in the first trial had been to avoid cross-examination, and cross-examination was now upon him. It was after 4 p.m. Schar was given the choice between beginning or waiting until after the weekend break.

He didn't hesitate: he wanted to begin.

The judge gave him one hour.

A visibly keyed-up Schar rose from his seat and immediately attacked. If "fucking golden" was the phrase heard around the world, then Schar's opening line was the question heard around the world.

"Mr. Blagojevich, you are a convicted liar, correct?" Schar asked, standing just a few feet away from Blagojevich.

It was on.

The courtroom erupted into a loud and chaotic scene, with Blagojevich's lawyers jumping up to object.

"Yes," Blagojevich blurted out, steamrolling over his lawyers.

Hands clasped behind his back, the tall, slim Schar inched toward a stern-faced Blagojevich. "It's fair to say, within hours of being convicted, you went and lied again," he said. This was a sore spot for the government. After Blagojevich was convicted on only one count out of 24 the year before, he marched downstairs to the courthouse lobby and gave a press conference where he lied again, in the government's view. That day, Blagojevich admitted he was convicted on a count involving his lying to an FBI agent in an interview. But he also told cameras that he was denied the opportunity to have a court reporter type up his responses.

That was a lie, Schar repeatedly said.

"I simply said that I did not lie to the FBI," Blagojevich answered from the stand. "That I answered every question honestly as I knew them, and I was not allowed a court reporter as I was told by my lawyers."

Schar was not going to let it go. He asked again: Why didn't Blagojevich tell the public that the FBI had actually offered to record the entire thing?

"You were the one who refused," Schar told him, jabbing his fingers toward Blagojevich and moving closer to him while the enraptured jury stared. The two sparred, talking over each other. Zagel tried to interject. Blagojevich's lawyers, too, were objecting, but their client ignored them and answered anyway.

Blagojevich wanted to communicate to the public that his conviction was unfair, Schar suggested. This was likely meant to affect those jurors who would decide his conviction.

"I had a strong opinion about it if you want to hear it," the ex-governor said. "This is why we have appellate courts...There's a process that will still unfold."

Schar said, "You wanted people to believe that the process that led to your conviction was unfair."

Blagojevich kept trying to slither out of Schar's verbal reach, reverting back to his old political self. He would pick only a part of the question to answer or simply say what he wanted, which had nothing to do with the question. The problem, though, was that now he was on the witness stand. In the past he had walked off TV sets when he didn't like the host's angle, or spoken from a script for a live news conference and then turned away without taking any questions. He could not do what he had done time after time in the years leading up to this testimony.

After 10 minutes of arguing, a stubborn Blagojevich finally answered, "I don't remember that."

The pitch in Schar's voice rose.

"Mr. Blagojevich," he replied, his voice dripping with sarcasm. Schar then pointed out what was obvious to everyone in that courtroom—that for five days of direct examination, Blagojevich gave hyper-detailed explanations about times, places, and dates of certain phone calls or exchanges—when they benefited him. Now that incredibly sharp memory failed him?

Jurors who had been taking studious notes earlier that day now had their pens down and their eyes glued to Schar. Schar moved around the courtroom quickly as he jumped from topic to topic, often mixing up the chronology of events, trying to knock Blagojevich off balance. Through the intense, rapid-fire questioning, Schar's voice alternately grew louder, higher, and often unquestionably sarcastic.

Schar asked Blagojevich if he ever revealed to the public that he was trying to get something for himself in exchange for the Senate seat.

"Ever tell the public you had your staff doing research on ambassadorships?"

"No," Blagojevich said.

Blagojevich talked over Schar and demanded more detailed questions, and called again for full transcripts of the recorded phone calls at the center of the government's case, as well as unedited video. It wasn't unlike what he'd do in his political life: deflect, distract, ask for more details, and ultimately not answer the question put to him.

Schar kept at it, demanding yes or no answers, and the judge repeatedly tried to steer Blagojevich back on track so he would answer the questions.

"I object to that," said Blagojevich—a onetime practicing lawyer—in response to one question. In response to another, he replied, "Asked and answered." At certain moments, three of Blagojevich's lawyers all objected at the same time to Schar's questions. Blagojevich ignored them and answered anyway.

"Judge, can we have a ruling?" one of Blagojevich's lawyers complained when objections were no longer acknowledged.

Zagel said Blagojevich was essentially acting as "his own lawyer" by plowing over their objections. In one such case, Zagel told a defense lawyer he was too late, wondering, "Are you objecting to his answer?" The judge later referred to "the relatively painful nature of what's happening in this courtroom."

Schar at one point zeroed in on an item Blagojevich had leaked to Michael Sneed, the *Sun-Times* gossip columnist, which said that Jackson had shot to the top of his Senate appointment list. Blagojevich said that he hadn't intended to appoint Jackson to the Senate, but wanted political operatives in Washington, D.C., to believe he was considering it.

"That was a lie," Schar said flatly.

"It was a misdirection play," Blagojevich replied.

"It was," Schar said in a snarky tone, "a lie. You thought you could get away with it because you thought no one would contradict you."

"I don't know that I thought that far ahead," Blagojevich said. "That was good politics. It's the quarterback faking a handoff and throwing long....It's part of the business."

Round and round the two went, and Blagojevich would not answer a question with a yes or no. Schar pointed to inconsistencies that leapt out during Blagojevich's public relations tour. In his book, Blagojevich had said he was ready on the morning before his arrest to name Lisa Madigan to the Senate seat; he even said he had directed his chief of staff, John Harris, to start doing the deal. But that directive was nowhere to be found in the relevant recordings of his calls with Harris.

Schar pulled out a copy of Blagojevich's book and read an excerpt regarding December 8, 2008. "'Over the phone,'" Schar read, "'I informed my chief of staff I had selected my first choice.'"

"That's not true," Schar said firmly.

"That is true," Blagojevich said.

"'Selected' her," Schar specified.

"She was my first choice," Blagojevich said. Schar asked Blagojevich to specify where in the transcripts he directed Harris to move on the Madigan deal. Blagojevich suggested the two could have met.

Schar and Blagojevich were jockeying to find their places in this verbal battle. Schar gradually grew less argumentative. Blagojevich, throughout, was repeatedly reminded to answer simply, with a yes or no. At the end of the day, with the jurors gone, Zagel asked how long the prosecution's cross-examination would take.

Schar said he had initially thought it would take a little more than one day, but now he wasn't so sure. "If it continues the way it's continued," Schar said on that June day, "the leaves will start turning."

The next week, Schar continued hammering the ex-governor with his own words on tape. Schar was trying to reinforce a theme: that Blagojevich repeatedly attempted to craft different deals for the Senate seat, but no one would bite. Both grew more calm and measured than they had been during that first fiery confrontation. Schar read back numerous recorded exchanges, including one where the ex-governor said he had the Senate seat "tightly wrapped in my arms."

"I'm willing to trade the thing I've got tightly held with her who doesn't have it held so tightly," he said on tape.

"You're the one who used the word 'trade,' isn't that right, Mr. Blagojevich?" Schar asked.

Then came a pivotal allegation: If Valerie Jarrett had been willing to make a deal with Blagojevich, "you would have named Jarrett senator," Schar said.

"I'm not sure what I would have done," Blagojevich insisted.

Schar finally relented after a day and a half of cross. His final question, though, was a simple one: Those were the ex-governor's words on tape, were they not?

Blagojevich replied, "Yes."

That day would end with Blagojevich stepping off the witness stand and doing something that, some would say, was classic Blagojevich: he tried to shake Schar's hand, right in front of the jury. Schar ignored him. Blagojevich even tapped Schar on the shoulder, but Schar didn't turn. Judge Zagel later told the jurors that prosecutors were not allowed to interact like that with defendants.

Closing arguments commenced, and the prosecution's reshuffling meant that Carrie Hamilton would now do the summation—the first part of the closing statements, which detailed each charge and explained how the government met its legal burden of proof. Hamilton focused on being clear and concise and explaining that the case, in reality, wasn't that difficult at all. She likely had in mind the fact that the jury in the first trial ended up complaining they were confused by the case.

A stoic Blagojevich sat up straight, hands folded, face blank, as Hamilton painted what she hoped would be a damning picture.

Hamilton told jurors that as they weighed the evidence, they needed only keep one question in mind: "Did the defendant try to get a benefit for himself in exchange for an official act?"

"That's really all this case and these charges boil down to, and it's really not any more complicated than that," Hamilton said.

Her closing argument addressed what had long been viewed as a weakness of the government's case—that Blagojevich was all talk and never actually completed the acts of which he was accused. Hamilton tried to hit home the point that it didn't matter whether the former governor was unsuccessful in getting something in exchange for the Senate seat appointment. The fact that he asked a union leader and friend of President-elect Obama about a cabinet position while considering Valerie Jarrett for the Senate seat was enough to break the law.

"The law protects people from being squeezed," Hamilton said. "The harm is done when the ask is made, because that's the violation of the people's trust."

"How do you know a scheme exists?" Hamilton asked jurors at one point. She lifted a hefty transcript of the calls. "Well, you got this."

Hamilton likened Blagojevich to a traffic cop who shakes down motorists for $50 after they're pulled over. Hamilton told jurors it would be "ludicrous" if that cop could only be held responsible when the motorist actually paid the bribe.

"But the defendant had so much more power than the traffic cop," she said. "He was the sitting governor of Illinois. He had a U.S. Senate seat. And it was effing golden."

She chided Blagojevich for his performance on the stand, telling jurors he lied to them repeatedly.

"This one's really good. Listen to him stammer," Hamilton told jurors as she discussed a December 4, 2008, call where Blagojevich said he was considering appointing Jackson. In this call, in which he tells advisers about the "tangible, political support" he could get "upfront," he is later heard on tape directing his brother to meet with Raghu Nayak. On the stand, Blagojevich admitted that Nayak's offer of $1.5 million for the Senate seat was "illegal."

Hamilton mocked Blagojevich's explanation: that he was simply telling his brother to meet with Nayak to relay that Jackson had better advance some good legislation—including a mortgage foreclosure bill—if he wanted the Senate seat. That explanation, she said, was a "whopper."

"He's the bribe guy. He's not the mortgage foreclosure guy," Hamilton said of Nayak, incredulously. "This is completely made up."

Hamilton told jurors not to be confused when Blagojevich said he wanted a political job in exchange for official action. That's still illegal, she said: "It's not just politics. This is a politician engaging in criminal conduct."

Up next was Goldstein. This was it for the defense. He quickly debunked Hamilton's corrupt cop analogy. There's never an instance when a police officer is allowed to take cash, he said. But a politician, well, that's a very different story.

Goldstein tore into the government witnesses, noting that they were given plea deals or immunity and were out to save themselves. He repeatedly hailed his client's decision to testify as "courageous" and reminded jurors that Blagojevich had absolutely no obligation to take the witness stand. He reminded jurors to focus on the former governor's intent as well as what he actually did—not just what he said—in terms of the alleged schemes.

Blagojevich did give Children's Memorial Hospital its funding. Despite the charge that Blagojevich would not advance proposed tollway improvements because he didn't get a campaign contribution, tollway executives did get $1.8 billion in state tollway money. The school in Rahm Emanuel's congressional district did get its state grant. And he appointed no one to the Senate seat before he was arrested—nor did he take a bribe from Jackson's emissaries before his arrest, Goldstein said.

At this, Goldstein's voice rose sharply.

"He didn't get a dime, a nickel, a penny," Goldstein said loudly and pointed across the room at Blagojevich. "He talked and he talked and that is all he did....They want you to believe his talk is a crime. It's not."

Goldstein asked jurors to focus on an instruction of law that allows politicians to ask for campaign contributions.

"We may not like the system. That is what we have," Goldstein said. "That is politics today, and that is the law." He asked jurors not to rubber-stamp Blagojevich "guilty" as the prosecution wanted.

"You see right there," Goldstein said, concluding his remarks by turning and pointing across the room at Blagojevich. "That's an innocent man. Right there, that's an innocent man."

As he drew the jury's eyes to his client, Patti began to cry, and the former governor grew teary eyed.

Despite the emotional remarks from the defense, though, it was Schar who had the last word. He repeatedly cut down the ex-governor's testimony, stacking up 11 government witnesses against the "convicted liar." He rebutted the defense's contention that the case was all talk.

"It's not that he talked too much and it means nothing," Schar said with biting sarcasm. "It's that he talked a lot and it means everything."

The prosecution was feeling confident, the defense hopeful. Each day that the jury was out, though, the feelings shifted. The judge imposed a gag order after Goldstein and Kaeseberg appeared on a local public television show about current events and after onetime Blagojevich attorney Sam Adam Jr. went on TV and radio predicting "20 not guilty verdicts" for his onetime client.

When the ninth day of jury deliberations concluded, the anxiety ramped up in the government camp. What was taking so long? Was there a holdout again?

On the tenth day, though, the jury delivered a note that it had reached a verdict on all but two counts. The decision seemed clear.

"He's toast," one lawyer close to the case declared privately. If jurors were fighting, they would have sent more notes asking for direction. The odds of the panel agreeing to acquit on 18 of 20 counts were astronomically slim.

Blagojevich arrived at a packed Dirksen courthouse that afternoon. Shaking hands with members of the media and greeting the spectators who ogled outside the courthouse—including construction workers across the street—Blagojevich stopped to ask a reporter how she had done in a weekend marathon. She said she had won.

"I hope I'm as lucky," he said. He held hands with his wife Patti, and the two headed upstairs to Zagel's courtroom on the 25th floor.

Patrick Fitzgerald, who had been criticized heavily since Blagojevich's mistrial the previous year, shuffled into the back of the courtroom to listen to the verdict. When he heard the jury's decision, Fitzgerald didn't betray a reaction.

Patti began to cry before the verdict was even read.

Count one: guilty. Count two: guilty. Count three: guilty. It was already clear—Blagojevich was going down hard.

The jury convicted him on 17 of 20 counts, including every count involving the sale of the Senate seat.

After the jury left, Patti stood up and buried her head in her husband's shoulder as he rubbed her back. The entire defense team looked numb. They lingered in the courtroom, wiping away tears.

After the crippling blow, it was unclear whether Blagojevich would face the cameras. The media waited and waited.

He did show up, at last. And finally, after years of proclaiming his innocence and fighting the charges with everything he had, Rod Blagojevich admitted defeat.

"Among the many lessons that I've learned from this whole experience is to try to speak a little bit less," Blagojevich told reporters after court, Patti at his side. "Patti and I obviously are very disappointed in the outcome. I, frankly, am stunned."

The government held a news conference.

Fitzgerald, Robert Grant of the FBI, and Tom Brady, head of the U.S. Postal Inspectors, were relieved, to say the least. No one wanted to confront the possibility of facing another mistrial. Calling it a "bittersweet moment," Fitzgerald referred to the conviction five years earlier of another former Illinois governor—George Ryan—who was still serving out his six-and-a-half-year sentence.

"Five years ago, another jury sent a message that corruption was not tolerable in Illinois politics. Governor Blagojevich did not get that message. I hope that message is heard this time," Fitzgerald said.

Fitzgerald bristled at the defense's contention that Blagojevich had been engaging in politics as usual when he was discussing the Senate seat sale on tape.

"That's not politics as usual," Fitzgerald said. "That's a crime."

"A famous artist once said Lady Justice is blind, but she has very sophisticated listening devices," said Grant. "There is no better evidence you can present to a jury than [a defendant's] own words in their own voice."

The difference between the two outcomes in the two different trials could not be overlooked. In the first trial, many jurors said they believed the prosecution's case against Blagojevich lacked a smoking gun. The following year's jury called the same evidence "overwhelming."

What changed?

Rod Blagojevich took the witness stand.

The eleven women and one man on his jury not only didn't buy what he said—they thought he was in full spin mode. Jury forewoman Connie Wilson, who was in her mid-50s, said she thought she recognized what Blagojevich was up to when he started picking and choosing details from his personal history. The details appeared to mirror personal information that came out when the judge questioned the jury pool before testimony began, she said.

"'Do you remember what he talked about…[while testifying about his home] library?'" Wilson said she asked other jurors during their deliberations. "He pointed to something in the library that pertained to almost everybody on the jury." She said jurors started piecing it together.

Over his seven days of testimony, Blagojevich mentioned books, targeting a librarian on the jury; pointed out an interest in music, directing the comment toward Wilson, the former choral director at Holy Spirit Catholic Community in Naperville; and discussed the importance of education, to connect with a teacher, Wilson said. "He even brought out at one point something about Boston, and of course our gentleman was a huge Boston fan," she said with a laugh, remembering the male juror's many Boston-themed T-shirts.

It was a monumental fall for the man who thought he could beat it all. Jurors who watched him testify for parts of seven days said they found him likable but ultimately not believable. Maribel DeLeon, a juror who often smiled at the ex-governor during his testimony, said she had wanted to side with Blagojevich. The evidence, though, did not side with him.

"I'd come in thinking, 'OK, he's not guilty,' and then all of a sudden I'm like, 'Gosh darn you, Rod! You did it again!'" said DeLeon, a mother of three. "He proved himself guilty beyond any reasonable doubt. He kept saying 'Do it.' 'Push it.' 'Get it done.' That's where he crossed the line."

The lone male in the group, John McParland, wasn't having any of Blagojevich's testimony. Particularly unconvincing, he said, was the ex-governor's attempt to explain what he "meant" by comments caught on tape by the government.

"You're talking in, like, two different languages, then?" McParland said in an interview.

The target-your-audience strategy may work with voters in politics, but it didn't fly with this group. It made juror Karen Wojcieszak downright angry.

"We had heard seven days of Mr. Blagojevich's 'blah, blah, blah,'" Wojcieszak said. "I don't care if he grew up poor on the North Side, of immigrant parents. We're all immigrants unless you're a Native American. He really cheated the people of Illinois, or tried to. He took an oath to do what was best for the people of Illinois and he didn't do it. So we'll have another governor in jail."

Even though they believed he was lying, many of the jurors still liked him.

"I almost feel like I'd want to apologize to him, but it's not my fault, so why do I have those feelings?" said Maya Moody. "Sometimes I think he was just surrounded by people that just didn't have the heart to speak the truth to him. It's either that or…that's just how the political machine in Illinois is, and he didn't think he was doing anything wrong. But, either way it goes, you know, when you look at the law…it was all illegal."

DeLeon described her decision to convict as "heartbreaking," particularly because Blagojevich, during his testimony, frequently mentioned his love for his wife and two daughters. His testimony did little to sway her views, she said. "His answers weren't consistent," she said. "There [were] many times it was clear he lied."

She said Blagojevich's own words, as secretly recorded by investigators, were critical in convincing her that Blagojevich had tried to extort campaign cash and was looking to benefit from trading the Senate seat.

"The tapes were very convincing," DeLeon said.

Deliberations had taken nearly 10 days because jurors had worked hard to keep their personal feelings about Blagojevich out of their discussions.

"We really followed the letter of the law," DeLeon said. "We kept going back to that, we were like 'this is exactly what it says; this is what we're going to do.' That's why it took so long."

"I believe Rod was out there helping the people," said DeLeon, who believes Blagojevich became "disgruntled" in office and started looking for a way out. "Everything was a snowball effect and he made poor choices," she said.

Jessica Hubinek, a 32-year-old librarian, wife, and mother, said that at about 3 p.m. on their ninth day of deliberations, she and her fellow jurors had decided that Blagojevich was guilty on 17 of the 20 counts. And in the spirit of the careful, deliberate way they had discussed, reviewed, and analyzed the evidence, they wanted to sleep on it and send their final decision to the judge Monday morning.

Rosemary Bennett, 73, said that the morning of the verdict she did something she had done every morning of the trial before that.

"I prayed every morning that the Lord would help each one of us jurors to base our decision on evidence and nothing else," she said. "It's easy to judge on preconceived notions."

The FBI's Grant said that, ultimately, Blagojevich was caught in unguarded moments on tape, "expressing his true desire, which was to personally profit from his public service."

"Perhaps the long national embarrassment of the State of Illinois over that last two and a half years has finally come to a conclusion," Grant said.

Chapter Fourteen

Going Away

In the run-up to his sentencing, Blagojevich did something new: he stopped talking. There were no more media interviews. He knew unless there were an appeal, the legal battle was over with respect to the charges. Now, he had to steady his focus on the sentencing guidelines. The former governor, continuing to amaze those close to him, believed he could get probation.

The prosecution, however, thought he qualified for up to a lifetime behind bars. Blagojevich had not apologized for his conduct even though he was repeatedly called on to do so.

Those close to him say Blagojevich was getting more distant from reality. But just before his sentencing, something happened that likely shook the former governor. His former fundraiser, Tony Rezko, whose name came up so often in Blagojevich's trial, was finally sentenced. It was three years after Rezko's conviction. He had cooperated, but only after he was convicted at trial. Prosecutors say Rezko hurt his value as a witness because he initially didn't tell prosecutors the extent of his wrongdoing.

U.S. District Judge Amy St. Eve leveled an incredible punishment—Rezko got 10½ years. It was one of the lengthiest terms ever seen for public corruption in Dirksen Federal Courthouse.

The next question on everyone's mind then was: If Rezko got 10½ years, what would Blagojevich get? Blagojevich was at the top of the scheme, and in the federal sentencing world, those at the top usually see the longest terms behind bars.

After Rezko's sentence, Blagojevich's lawyers simply asked the judge to be lenient, given his good works as governor and the fact that he had two school-aged daughters.

But those who believed Judge St. Eve had set the bar turned out to be right. Rod Blagojevich's sentencing hearing was held in the Dirksen Federal Courthouse's ceremonial courtroom, the largest in that building, to accommodate all the spectators. It took two days, and the former governor spoke on the second day. Minutes before he was to learn his fate, Blagojevich joked with reporters. He called out to Mary Ann Ahern, a political reporter for WMAQ-TV, asking her about her kids, remembering their names and ages. When Ahern said one of her kids was interested in political science, Blagojevich scoffed. He told her to let him know if she wanted him to convince her kids not to make that move, and laughed as he headed back to his seat.

When it came time for him to address the judge, Blagojevich stood up, turned back to Patti, touched her hand, and whispered, "I love you." He then stood at a lectern in the center of the giant courtroom. Over 20 minutes, in a low, somber voice that sometimes cracked with emotion, Blagojevich said he took responsibility for his crimes. It was the first time he had made such an admission.

"I have nobody to blame but myself for my stupidity and actions and the things I did and I thought I could do. I'm not blaming anybody. I've accepted all of it," Blagojevich said in a voice low and devoid of its usual animation.

The courtroom fell quiet as Blagojevich spoke. At times, it grew so hushed that the only sounds were his voice and the scribbling of pens on paper.

"The jury convicted me," the former governor continued. "They convicted me because those were my actions...I caused it all. I'm not blaming anybody. I was the governor, and I should have known better."

Blagojevich apologized to the state; to his onetime codefendant brother; to his two daughters, now 15 and 8; and to his wife, Patti, whom he said stood by him through the worst of times.

"[Because of] my stupidity and my mistakes and things I've talked about and discussed, my children have had to suffer," Blagojevich said. "I've ruined their innocence. They have to face the fact when they go out into the world that their father is a convicted felon, and it's not like their name is Smith, and they can hide."

Blagojevich left the lectern red-eyed and teary after his address to Zagel, who stared back at him plainly, at times taking notes. He walked over to kiss Patti on the head. She had a pained look on her face. The judge ordered a break, and chatter started back up in the courtroom. Blagojevich stood with Patti and his lawyers. He rubbed Patti's back while they waited.

When Zagel returned to the bench, it was clear he was unlikely to show much mercy.

"When it is the governor who goes bad, the fabric of Illinois is torn and disfigured and not easily or quickly repaired," Zagel said. "The harm here is not measured in the value of money or property...The harm is the erosion of public trust in government.... You did that damage."

Even taking into account the somber apology from the former governor, Zagel announced his sentence: 14 years in prison.

Blagojevich, who was seated with his feet crossed and hands clasped as Zagel read his sentence, slightly lowered his head after learning his prison term. Patti put her hand up to her mouth, but did not cry as she had at previous hearings.

The term was two years more than the term the same judge gave a cooperating mobster who had killed 14 people. It was one of the stiffest sentences in Illinois history for any political corruption conviction. Zagel delivered the harsh term even after factoring in that Blagojevich had accepted responsibility with an apology that many doubted would ever come.

After learning his fate, Blagojevich whispered to his wife, "You OK? Stay strong." The two later embraced in the courtroom, and Patti Blagojevich buried her head in her husband's chest.

The once-popular Illinois governor, who had promised reform after the scandals of his predecessor George Ryan, now faced more than twice as much time in prison. Prosecutors had wanted even more. Schar had asked for 15 to 20 years in prison, saying that Blagojevich was manipulative and had spent seven days on the witness stand during his trial perjuring himself.

"He tried to lie his way out of a guilty verdict," he said. "He is incredibly manipulative, and he knows how to be. To his credit, he is clever about it." Schar asked Zagel to send a message when sentencing Blagojevich.

"A message must be sent to the people of Illinois that when they are victimized by corruption, their frustration, their disappointment, their cynicism, their disenfranchisement from political process—they're being heard," Schar said. "The people have had enough. They have had enough of this defendant. They have had enough of people like him."

After the sentence was imposed, Fitzgerald called it "profoundly sad." Having two Illinois governors convicted of crimes in the same century was too many, he said.

"We've seen it happen twice in five years," Fitzgerald said. "The public has had enough, and judges have had enough," Fitzgerald said, referring to the 14-year sentence. "This needs to stop. To put it very, very simply, we don't want to be back here again."

After the sentence was announced, dozens of people stood still throughout the federal courthouse lobby. They stared toward the elevators, hoping to catch a glimpse of the former governor.

The public seemed divided on the sentence. Many thought it was far too harsh for Blagojevich, given that the government did not prove he pocketed money. Others felt it was overdue.

At the time, one legal expert said he was shocked by the sentence.

"I think it's outrageous," said DePaul law professor Len Cavise. He likened the prison term to cruel and unusual punishment. "The judge and the prosecution went off the deep end on this one."

Federal authorities thought differently.

"Our investigation and the evidence collected during the investigation proved that corruption was taking place," FBI Special Agent Dan Cain said in a podcast produced by the FBI. "The judge in the sentencing hearing was sending a clear message that corruption would not be tolerated in our government in Illinois, so we believe that we did our job."

Chapter Fifteen

"Blago Has Left the Balcony"

The buzzing started early that day.

Helicopters chopped furiously at the air over the otherwise quiet Northwest Side neighborhood on March 14, 2012, in Chicago. The weather was pushing 80 degrees, and maybe it was that record warmth that drew so many people to 2934 W. Sunnyside. It was Rod Blagojevich's final night of freedom. The Ravenswood Manor home where Blagojevich spent so much of his time as governor, the place where FBI agents tapped his phone and then arrested him, would once again hold some public significance.

For Blagojevich's last meal at home later that Wednesday night, Patti cooked a spaghetti dinner, using Blagojevich's late mother's recipe. "I'm going to eat so much spaghetti I won't need breakfast," he said.

For his youngest daughter, Annie, Blagojevich left as a memento two dolls that have the capability to play back recorded messages. According to someone close to the family, one of the recordings is Blagojevich's voice saying, "Hi, Annie. Daddy loves you."

On this day, staring at 14 years in prison, the former governor promised he'd talk publicly one last time. As he had in the past, he timed his remarks for 5:02 p.m.—correctly predicting that TV channels would carry them live.

This promised to be his last public statement for perhaps more than a decade. His term loomed at the Federal Correctional Institution, Englewood, a low-security federal prison in Denver's southwest suburbs. A judge had recommended he enter a substance abuse program that would help shave time off his sentence. Still, Blagojevich faced the prospect of not getting out of prison until he turned 67.

As the afternoon wore on, the Blagojeviches' front yard transformed into an outrageous circus of media and misfits. Even with two hours remaining before his remarks, giant TV antennae protruded above treetops on side streets. Chicago police squad cars circled the neighborhood and eventually parked outside the home.

A banner hanging from the railing of the Blagojevich home read, "Thanks, Mr. Governor. We will pray." Another cardboard sign taped to the railing read, "Good luck, Mr. Rod. Your [sic] a good man and we know you got cheated. Never give up and keep the faith."

In the midst of this, Blagojevich left his home briefly for an outing with Annie. Reporters and photographers converged on them as they made their way to their car. When they returned, an even bigger crowd of reporters closed on dad and daughter, who tried to snake their way back to their home. His hand on his daughter, Blagojevich smiled but wouldn't give interviews. "Ask questions later!" shouted Annie to the crowd, holding a pink bag that had the words "Sweet and Sassy" on it. Blagojevich bent toward his daughter excitedly.

"That's it, excellent job!" Blagojevich told her as they walked inside. "That's my girl!"

The crowd outside grew and grew. A group of people carrying "FREE BLAGO" signs and twin poster boards with "BLAGO" on one and "JEVICH" on the other seemed to show up around the same time. Dads put children on their shoulders. Moms pushing strollers stopped for a peek.

One gentleman who fancied himself "security"—though he clearly wasn't—announced he wanted supporters to hold hands and form a human wall that the media could not cross. He offered to "deputize" anyone who would step forward and help Blagojevich talk to the pubic with "some dignity."

"Let's help Rod Blagojevich take back the sidewalk!" he yelled. People did step up and hold hands, raising tensions between the members of the public and the members of media who had been gathering.

When Rod and Patti finally emerged from their home, the crowd cheered. The couple walked down the balcony and into the thick of the crowd, heading toward cameras stationed at the far end of the front lawn. The crowd inched along with the Blagojeviches, shouting questions. Through a tangle of camera wires, video camera people walked backward, as did some supporters and reporters. The couple stopped at a bank of microphones near another crowd. The first crowd kept moving, even though there was no place to go. People trampled one another, stepping on each other's feet, knocking one another off balance. It was a raucous, if not dangerous, scene—a staggering mix of people, personalities, and energy crammed onto the former governor's front lawn.

Cindy Hicks, 53, who said she lived in the neighborhood, said she thought Blagojevich would face a tough psychological challenge being locked up, but she added, "He's charming enough that I'm sure he'll make friends in there."

Gloria Leverence, 70, who was there to hear the former governor speak, said she came to see "history." She said she had asked her grandchildren to come, but they told her she was "crazy." Leverence also said she felt like the ex-governor needed her support.

"I have three grandchildren who have free healthcare because of him," Leverence said. "I liked riding the bus for free for all these years....I don't think he deserved what he got....He didn't kill anyone."

"If he was found guilty, he was probably guilty," said Elizabeth Sage, 31, who was out for a stroll with her 9-month-old son and stopped to watch. "I'm glad to see an end to the circus, but as soon as he's gone, another circus will start—but hopefully just not around here."

With dozens of photographers, video cameras, and supporters all around him, Blagojevich slung his arm around his wife. His fingernails appeared chewed on. Blagojevich held onto Patti through his 12-minute statement, squeezing her shoulder tightly at times. He bid adieu to Illinois, talking about "a dark and hard journey" that would take him thousands of miles from his family.

"How do you make sense of all this? What do you tell your children when calamity strikes and hardship comes? What do you do when disaster hits your family, and you leave behind your children and your wife?" Blagojevich asked. "Tomorrow, saying goodbye to Patti and my kids will be the hardest thing I've ever had to do. I've been putting off the thought about what that's going to be like. I can't even think about it now."

As Blagojevich spoke, a man carrying an American flag tried to break through a gap in the crowd, knocking others off balance as he attempted to find space where there was none. He kept yelling, "Governor! Governor!"

A deeply tanned, blonde newswoman swore at him, telling him to get back.

"Stop it! He's not going to take it!" she snapped.

"I have to confess," Blagojevich went on with his speech. "There are times that I want to give up."

Meanwhile, the man in the crowd didn't relent. He pushed and shoved his way closer to Blagojevich and eventually draped an American flag over the former governor's and Patti's shoulders.

"Governor! Esteban!" the man said, identifying himself. "See, he took it. He took it."

Blagojevich was talking at the moment the flag was draped over them. He and Patti seemed startled and looked back at their shoulders. Someone quickly snapped it off them.

"It has been, walking through life with Patti, a most gracious journey," Blagojevich went on. "And you know when she took her vow when we were married and she said through good times and bad, neither one of us could ever have imagined it would be like this. And here's been Patti, standing strong, and standing tall."

Patti, wearing a thin layer of makeup and dressed simply in a purple shirt and blue jeans, broke down. She passed her hand over her eyes to wipe away tears that she could no longer blink back.

His remarks veered into vintage Blagojevich, again bringing up the All Kids insurance program, free mass-transit rides for senior citizens, and the fact that he never raised the income tax.

"I got bruised and battered and bloodied, but we were able to get those done," he said. Blagojevich again called his words on tape "political talk" and "horse-trading"—characterizations that prosecutors had repeatedly taken issue with.

"I believed I was on the right side of the law," he said. "The decision went against me."

For a moment in the statement, Blagojevich seemed to second-guess his actions over the preceding three years. The TV appearances, the news conferences that thumbed a nose at prosecutors—maybe they weren't such a good idea after all.

"Maybe one of the lessons of this whole story is that you got to be maybe a little bit more humble. You can never have enough humility," he said. "Maybe I could have had more of that."

Within minutes of these words leaving his lips, Blagojevich walked away from the microphones and began signing autographs. As he made his way back to his house, he pointed to people in the crowd. Shook hands. Punched his fist in the air.

"Rod, will you still give speeches from prison?" one young man shouted, laughing. Across the crowd, a school-age boy also laughed, and his father scolded him, "It's not a joking matter."

"Hey, I got on three different [TV] stations," the boy said proudly. "That's pretty good."

Back on his balcony, Blagojevich crouched through the iron bars to reach people or sign autographs. The more he signed, the more random items people passed to him. He refused nothing: posters, papers, school notebooks, a Girl Scout cookie box, T-shirts, receipts, hats. One person handed him a CTA card. Another handed up a torn, yellow M&Ms wrapper.

"Oh that's so nice of him! Oh, look, he's signing that too. That's so nice of him!" one woman exclaimed. As if he were on stage, Blagojevich picked up a young girl out of the crowd and lifted her over the bars and onto the balcony with him. She beamed. He did the same later with at least two other children.

Annie Blagojevich came outside three times, trying to lure her father back into the house for the last night he'd spend there. She asked him to stop signing autographs. He'd look to her, then to the crowd.

He couldn't help himself. He stayed outside.

Celebrity washed over Rod Blagojevich, and however minor it was, he reveled in it. This strange chapter in Chicago political history ended with Blagojevich acting more like a preening rock star than a disgraced politician heading off to prison. He ignored the questions from the usual shouting print reporters but began giving mini-interviews to Spanish TV stations. In Spanish, he ticked off the same political stump talk he used to give in English. The reporters ate it up.

Apparently running out of words he knew in the foreign language, he shouted: *"Viva Chivas!,"* a reference to a revered *futbol* club in Mexico. And he shouted another common refrain: *"Si se puede!"* A woman in the scrum yelled back, *"Si se puede! SI SE PUEDE!!"*

The ridiculousness factor reached its height.

If Blagojevich's actions were bizarre for a man heading to prison, they were arguably eclipsed by those of well-wishers showering adoration onto a convicted felon, begging for his autograph. Not to mention the media, which flooded the neighborhood with helicopters, reporters, and equipment, helping to create the spectacle, and then bringing it live to their audience.

As he finally closed out his interaction with the crowd, Blagojevich stretched hard over his balcony, balancing on the tops of his thighs, his feet in the air, as he reached out to people below. He swept the tops of their hands with his fingertips.

With the ex-governor finally inside, the crowd thinned, and some of the news media retreated. It was then that a *Sun-Times* reporter, Stefano Esposito, found something on the ground.

"I saw this get passed up to him," he said. It was the yellow M&Ms wrapper. In black ink over the torn paper, a signature was scrawled: Rod R. Blagojevich.

The next day, Blagojevich left early for Colorado, and the media again was on top of him. Reporters bought tickets and flew on the same flight. They filmed the ex-governor in the airport going through security. They filmed his car as it drove on the highway toward the prison. The prison wasn't quite ready for him and asked him to come back a little later, his lawyer said. He was driven to lunch, and the media followed, launching conspiracy theories that he had second thoughts about reporting to prison.

Eventually, Blagojevich did make it inside. Aaron Goldstein and Shelly Sorosky escorted their client all the way there. Then they left. The prison door shut.

The silence was likely deafening.

That same day, this reporter appeared on CNN to talk about Blagojevich.

The anchor said she had struggled to find the "deeper meaning" in all of this, but couldn't. Was there a deeper meaning, she asked?

If there was one, it was difficult to pinpoint. In all, 15 people were convicted in Operation Board Games, including two former chiefs of staff for Blagojevich. Blagojevich's attempt at humility, such as it was, fell flat. Deterrence? The day before Blagojevich gave his farewell address, and months after his lengthy sentence was imposed, an Illinois state lawmaker named Derrick Smith, a Democrat from Chicago's West Side, was arrested three days after he allegedly took a $7,000 bribe.

There were tapes.

Smith refused to resign, and a week after he was handcuffed, he was reelected. He carried 77 percent of the vote.

Two weeks before that, Cook County Commissioner William Beavers was charged with misusing his campaign fund. Beavers, too, refused to resign. At a news conference, he thumbed his nose at prosecutors.

Beavers and Smith had another thing in common: they hired Sam Adam Jr. as their attorney.

The judge that Beavers randomly drew? James Zagel.

With that, the Chicago Machine churned.

Epilogue

In the year between the writing of this book and its print publication, the cauldron of Chicago corruption continued to boil, and what bubbled to the surface was one Jesse Jackson Jr.

The storyline for the oldest son of the national civil rights leader unfolded in a way that no one could have imagined.

A few months after Blagojevich headed to the big house with great fanfare, Jackson disappeared from the U.S. House in the dark of night.

The public would not learn the congressman was missing in action until two weeks later. His office put out a news release saying he was suffering from exhaustion and was on medical leave.

Of course, the antennae of every cynic in Chicago shot up.

Jackson's announcement showed some calculation. It was timed for 5 p.m. on the day of the deadline for candidates to file to challenge him in the fall election.

Right around that time, someone else from the Blagojevich storyline fell.

Raghuveer Nayak—the Jackson confidant and donor who had leveled accusations against Jackson to the FBI in the Blagojevich case—was arrested on federal charges.

Nayak's troubles, it turned out, were unrelated to Blagojevich. The wealthy owner of surgical centers in Illinois and Indiana was accused of running a kickback scheme with doctors who operated out of his buildings. Still, Nayak's appearance in Chicago's federal court sounded alarms.

Did Jackson disappear because he knew about Nayak and feared he would talk? That didn't make sense, of course, because Nayak had already talked to authorities about Jackson on the subject of the Senate seat allegations.

One of Jackson's lawyers, Paul Langer, told the *Sun-Times* that Jackson's absence unequivocally had nothing to do with Nayak. Jackson himself, though, stayed underground and out of sight.

Then *Sun-Times* columnist Michael Sneed broke the news that Jackson had been admitted to Mayo Clinic in Minnesota. The Jackson family released a statement through Mayo saying Jackson suffered from bipolar disorder and was undergoing treatment.

His wife, Chicago Alderman Sandi Jackson of the 7th Ward, began suggesting that Jackson might not return until after the November election. There was a behind-the-scenes campaign to get out the word that Jackson was severely depressed and could barely function.

Soon after, the online scandal sheet Gawker broke a story saying that Jackson Jr. had been spotted at a bar in Washington, D.C. , drinking and hanging out with women who were not his wife. Severe scrutiny—and criticism—of the political power couple intensified.

There were questions about how Alderman Sandi Jackson could adequately serve her ward while living in Washington, D.C. The couple's children attended an elite private school in Washington, D.C.—not Chicago. Questions also surfaced over the fact that Sandi was getting paid $5,000 a month from her husband's congressional fund, and sometimes more, for being a "campaign manager." Jackson, clearly, was not campaigning.

In September of that year, the Jacksons brought on more scrutiny after putting their home in the Dupont Circle neighborhood of Washington, D.C., on the market. The asking price: $2.5 million. Observers wondered how the Jacksons could afford that home, their second, on their publicly paid salaries. They had purchased it for $575,000 in 1998, just a few years after Jackson first came to Washington. It was far from a humble crash pad. It boasted two kitchens, four bedrooms, five fireplaces, and a rooftop Jacuzzi.

Those close to Jackson insisted the "for sale" sign had nothing to do with Jackson's political future.

"Like millions of Americans, Congressman Jackson and Mrs. Jackson are grappling with soaring health care costs and are selling their residence to help defray costs of their obligations," a statement from his office read.

Sandi Jackson told others her husband still planned to campaign "vigorously" for reelection.

"I can't speak to when that's going to happen or how that's going to happen," she said at the time. "I can only say that I will continue to rely on [doctors'] expertise. I would only ask for patience."

But it turned out that in addition to his medical woes, Jesse Jackson Jr. was also suffering from something else: a severe case of federal scrutiny. As in Nayak's case, it had nothing to do with Blagojevich.

In October 2012, this *Sun-Times* reporter called Jackson's loyal longtime Washington press secretary Frank Watkins to inform him the paper was about to break a story indicating it had confirmed Jackson was under criminal investigation for suspicious activity in his campaign fund.

The news appeared to stun Watkins, who responded with a long, silent pause over the phone. He then asked me to repeat the statement.

Watkins explained he wasn't in regular contact with Jackson and didn't even have a phone number to reach him.

Less than a month before the November 6, 2012, election, news of the investigation spread quickly, and more reports with more details followed. Jackson didn't campaign or show himself publicly. But he also didn't drop out of the race. Instead, he released a robo-call in the district asking for constituents' patience—and their votes.

Without even showing up, he cruised to reelection.

Fifteen days later, he resigned. In his resignation letter, he acknowledged the federal probe for the first time.

The following January, Sandi Jackson resigned her position as alderman.

On February 20, 2013, Jesse Jackson Jr. and his wife entered a Washington, D.C., courthouse to do something that was becoming almost routine for Chicago politicians. Both were admitting their guilt to federal charges.

During all the years that Jackson Jr. had so vehemently protested any association with the Blagojevich corruption, the congressman and his wife were elbow-deep in the cookie jar.

The two pleaded guilty to the scheme of making $750,000 in improper purchases out of their campaign fund over seven years. The Jackson name held much clout in Chicago's 2nd District, which is heavily African American, allowing him to easily sail to reelection many times over his 17-year career.

He also easily raised money. It poured in from unions and big companies, and it poured in from some residents of lesser means in his district, who likely hoped the Jackson name would bolster their communities.

In fact, Jackson's district included some of the most crime-ridden and poor areas in the state. Just steps from Jesse and Sandi

Jackson's South Side campaign office, which boasted life-sized photos of the couple plastered to window panels, stood building after building boarded up due to foreclosures.

Even though Jackson rarely faced opposition in his elections, his campaign fund was regularly drained, according to government charges. In violation of federal election laws, the campaign money went toward bankrolling a high-end lifestyle for both Jacksons.

The items they bought were as over-the-top as some of the expenditures described in undercover FBI recordings of Blagojevich.

In 2007, Jesse Jackson Jr. bought a $43,000 gold Rolex watch with money from his campaign fund. In 2007 and 2008, he bought nearly $10,000 in Bruce Lee memorabilia.

Then there was the $3,900 Michael Jackson hat, the $4,000 Michael Jackson and Eddie Van Halen guitar, the $5,000 football signed by American presidents, and the mounted elk heads. All were bought with campaign money. Sandi Jackson sold them back to undercover FBI agents and deposited the proceeds into a personal bank account.

They jetted off to Disney World and sent family members on a holistic retreat in Martha's Vineyard.

They even used the campaign money to buy toothpaste, underwear, and toilet paper.

These purchases were made before and after Blagojevich's spectacular arrest. The Jacksons embezzled even after the FBI sat down with the congressman for an interview on the true nature of his involvement in the Blagojevich case.

In one day in 2009, Jesse and Sandi Jackson dipped into campaign money to make four purchases at Edwards-Lowell Furrier and Fur Shop in Beverly Hills. According to the federal indictment, the Jacksons dropped $800 on a mink cashmere cape, $1,500 on a black-and-red cashmere cape, $1,200 on a mink reversible parka, and $1,500 on a "black fox reversible." They had it all shipped to their Washington, D.C., home.

They spent more than $15,000 of campaign money at Abt Electronics on a washer and dryer, a range, and a refrigerator for their home in Chicago and spent more than $30,000 in campaign money to renovate their Washington, D.C., home.

According to the indictment, the Jacksons used a credit card to cover up these purchases. They lied on federal election reports about the nature of the expenditures. Working through a staffer, they also mislabeled purchases; in one case, Jackson Jr. labeled an expense as a room rental for a campaign event, when in fact he had purchased porcelain collectibles.

The indictment went on to say that Jackson outright laundered money using a staff member, and that in 2011, he leaned on an unnamed person to pay $25,000 on one of his and his wife's credit cards.

The conduct was flagrant and far-reaching. The FBI-led investigation had shown that over seven years, the Jacksons engaged in more than 3,100 transactions for their personal gain. It was all too much for Jackson to explain to a jury. Had Jackson gone to trial, much more of his dirty laundry would have been aired. He might have had to answer even more incredibly uncomfortable questions.

"The nature of this spending makes clear this was not a momentary lapse of judgment," said U.S. Attorney Ronald C. Machen Jr. "This was not a short streak of impulsive behavior."

In February 2013, Jesse Jackson Jr. was in court to enter a guilty plea. In the courtroom, Jackson began blinking back tears before the judge even reached the bench. Sandi Jackson sat in the front row, her husband occasionally turning to her from the front of the room.

More details were surfacing about a falling out between Sandi Jackson and her husband's family, particularly between her and the Reverend Jesse Jackson. This was likely why Jackson Jr.'s parents sat a row behind Sandi in court, along with their other family members. The Reverend Jackson was often the first to step up to cameras in any given city, on a variety of issues. On this day, he had no comment.

Ever the politician, Jackson Jr. made his plea in the courtroom predictably dramatic.

In the middle of the proceedings, his lawyer had to grab tissues from a box and hand them to his crying client.

Jackson wiped tears from his face when the judge discussed the possibility of prison time. He was asked if he understood he was waiving his right to a jury trial.

"In perfect candor, Your Honor, I have no interest in wasting the taxpayers' time or their money," Jackson said.

"Sir, for years I lived in my campaign. I used monies that should have been used for campaign purposes, and I used them for myself personally, to benefit me personally," Jackson continued. "And I am acknowledging that that which the government has presented is accurate."

The judge asked if Jackson wanted to consult with his lawyer once more before he answered the "ultimate question."

Jackson paused, then turned around and looked back at his wife. She gave him the go-ahead.

"Ask the question," he said dramatically.

Do you plead guilty? the judge asked.

"I am guilty, Your Honor."

Afterward, Jackson told the media to send word to the district where he hadn't made a public appearance for more than six months.

"Tell everybody back home I'm sorry I let them down, OK?" Jackson said.

However, his top attorney, Reid Weingarten, later made clear that a battle was still to come at sentencing.

Weingarten said there would be a substantial presentation at sentencing to try to persuade the judge that the congressman should get a break because of a serious medical condition.

"That's not an excuse, that's just a fact," Weingarten said.

Weingarten was referring to a previous Jackson family statement saying the congressman had bipolar disorder. But a reporter jumped in, clearly not buying it.

"He's a shopping addict?" asked WGN-TV's Julie Unruh.

Weingarten did not answer her question, or anyone else's.

In the news conference that followed the couple's guilty pleas, Machen, the U.S. Attorney in Washington, D.C.'s federal district seemed to convey a level of personal disappointment.

Machen echoed what so many were saying in Washington that day: Jackson swapped his incredible potential to lead people and change their lives for a focus on extreme indulgences that were foreign to many people living in his district.

"The guilty plea today is so tragic because it represents such wasted potential. Jesse Jackson Jr. had the drive, the ability, and the talent to be the voice of a new generation. But he squandered that talent, exchanged that instead to satisfy his personal whims and his extravagant lifestyle," Machen said.

During that news conference, IRS and FBI officials touched on similar themes. Public corruption may persist, but so too would investigations of those elected to office.

No one, they said, was above the laws of this land—not even those who made them.

Acknowledgments

I was about five days away from giving birth to my second son in December 2011, when I received a phone call from Agate publisher Doug Seibold. We had met years earlier at a journalism event. Seibold had kept my business card all those years and, to my surprise, remembered our conversation almost verbatim. He encouraged me to write a book, telling me that I was the one to tell this story. I thank him for his faith in me.

I'd be remiss if I didn't recognize a known fact in Chicago: this is one of the best towns in the nation for news because it has some of the most dogged reporters in the country. Investigative work by Dave McKinney, Chris Fusco, and Tim Novak at the *Sun-Times* not only exposed schemes under Blagojevich but unearthed information that ended up in Blagojevich's indictment. Bulldog City Hall reporter Fran Spielman got Dick Mell to spill what would turn out to be one of the most memorable airings of a family's dirty laundry in Chicago political history. My editors at the *Sun-Times*—Don Hayner, Shamus Toomey, Paul Saltzman, and Scott Fornek—were there with constant direction and wisdom. Sarah Ostman and Lark Turner, my interns for Blagojevich trials one and two, respectively, produced amazing work and kept me sane, while political reporter Abdon Pallasch parachuted in when I needed him. Thank you to *Sun-Times* Washington Bureau Chief Lynn Sweet, who provided critical guidance on the blog. Competitors from other media outlets, including the crews of local TV and radio, and, particularly, reporters with the *Chicago Tribune*, were worthy adversaries throughout and played a role in exposing corruption under Blagojevich.

The indefatigable Randall Samborn at the U.S. Attorney's office, and Ross Rice at the FBI, worked to make a reporter's job easier.

A personal thanks to my supportive neighbors and family, especially my sisters, Alexandra and Lisa, as well as my other family, the McCoppins, for their ongoing support. And to my mother-in-law, Rose Marie McCoppin, who loyally reads my stories in the *Sun-Times* and is an ever-faithful supporter of my work.

Thank you to my parents, Adela and Eduardo Korecki, who not only guide me in life but are always there with a loving smile and embrace for their grandkids. To my husband, Bob McCoppin, who is my rock and whom I turn to for his eternal wisdom.

My youngest son, Cormac, held off his entrance into life until just a week after the governor's sentencing. (We cut it so close that Patti Blagojevich herself asked me at the sentencing to make my water break just to get her out of there.) To my oldest son, Daniel, who not only showed amazing patience as his mom tapped away at the keyboard into the wee hours of the morning, but constantly reminded me what life is really about.

A young Rod Blagojevich, pictured here in February 2002 during his first run for the governor's office. (Photo by Bob Black, reprinted with permission from the *Chicago Sun-Times*)

An avid runner, Blagojevich was often seen darting through Chicago neighborhoods. Here, he runs with longtime friend and confidant Lon Monk, who would eventually cooperate in the government's case against Blagojevich. (Photo by Scott Stewart, reprinted with permission from the *Chicago Sun-Times*)

Rod Blagojevich is caught in the media scrum after pleading not guilty to a criminal federal indictment in 2009. (Photo by Brian Jackson, reprinted with permission from the *Chicago Sun-Times*)

Blagojevich is lost in a sea of cameras on the day of his arraignment in Chicago federal court. (Photo by John White, reprinted with permission from the *Chicago Sun-Times*)

U.S. Rep. Jesse Jackson Jr. (right), with his father the Reverend Jesse Jackson (center) and his wife, Chicago Alderman Sandi Jackson, at a Jackson Foundation event in 2006. The congressman was not charged in the Blagojevich case, but embarrassing revelations emerged about his involvement in the scandal. (Photo by John Sall, reprinted with permission from the *Chicago Sun-Times*)

Stuart Levine leaves the Dirksen Federal Building in April 2008. Levine, a political power broker with many secrets to hide, became a major cooperator in the investigation. (Photo by Richard A. Chapman, reprinted with permission from the *Chicago Sun-Times*)

Christopher Kelly, Blagojevich's friend and a major fundraiser, was indicted three times. Here he leaves the federal courthouse on September 8, 2009, just days before he would take his own life. (Photo by Richard A. Chapman, reprinted with permission from the *Chicago Sun-Times*)

The day before reporting to prison in March 2012, Rod Blagojevich and a distraught Patti Blagojevich address the media and dozens of onlookers outside their Chicago home. (Photo by Scott Stewart, reprinted with permission from the *Chicago Sun-Times*)

F

During his legal saga, Blagojevich sometimes arrived in court to cheers and hugs from supporters. (Photo by John H. White, reprinted with permission from the *Chicago Sun-Times*)

Tony Rezko, eventually convicted of corruption for his role in the Blagojevich scandal, was once also a fundraiser for Barack Obama. (Photo by John H. White, reprinted with permission from the *Chicago Sun-Times*)

Rod Blagojevich smiling
and signing autographs
outside his Chicago home
the day before leaving for
prison in March 2012.
(Photo by John J. Kim,
reprinted with permission
from the *Chicago Sun-
Times*)

H

CPSIA information can be obtained
at www.ICGtesting.com
Printed in the USA
LVHW011140120920
665577LV00005B/133